Hello and welcome to
evolve over 22 years
Valley with my family
activity guide that the n

MW01444306

families can really enjoy while visiting our wonderful and scenic Banff, Canmore and surrounding areas. This guide book isn't written with the "*Über outdoors person*" in mind. Instead it's meant to be lighthearted and fun. I've geared it to those looking for Rocky Mountain excursions that don't require a huge drive, heavy backpack, sore feet or kids forever whining *"are we there yet?"* And, it's small and light enough to carry with you wherever you go.

Many of the excursions listed in *Out'n About* are short, half day adventures that only locals know about. They are easy to find and navigate without any guesswork. Most are free, but some guided or tour excursions I've highlighted do have fees.

I'm so glad to be sharing our experiences with you. Thanks for buying this book – open it up and take a look!

Out'n About Banff & Canmore

A fun & friendly guide by local Donna Scott

Spring/Summer/Fall 2012 - Second Edition

Dedication

To Robin, Kimberly and Geoff for urging me on to write this guide. To the hapless goat who's leg is still hanging from the tree at Cougar Creek. To Scott Cook, author of *Curious Gorge*, who has been a huge inspiration. And, a big thanks to all my extended family and friends who continue to enjoy coming out with us on our adventures and have helped contribute immensely to this book! A pat for Socks 'n Guinness too.

Second Edition © 2012 by the author of this book (Donna Scott). Donna retains sole copyright to her contributions to this book.

Exploration, text and photography by Donna Scott (or her friends & relatives photos).

Cover photo: A signature Three Sisters Mountain view along with various activities in Banff and Canmore.

What's That??

An Inuksuk (pronounced "Inookshook") is a stone figure that was originally built by the Inuit native peoples of Arctic Canada, Alaska and Greenland. "Inuksuk" is the Inuktitut term used to refer to these figures. It means "to act in the capacity of a human" and is an extension of the word inuk, which translates as "a human being." Inuksuk were placed upon the landscape for different reasons. The Inuit used them as hunting and navigational aids, coordination points, markers and message centers. The stone figure appears on the Canadian Territory flag of Nunavut and was the graphical symbol used for the Vancouver 2010 Winter Olympics.

You'll see these cheery characters helping to guide you all over the Rocky Mountains, making sure travelers find their way. Be sure to build one of your own.

A Few Notes From the Author

Although the information in this book has been checked by the author and her friends and family for accuracy and she performs daily weather dances for your benefit, #@%* happens. Trail conditions can change quickly and weather in the Rocky Mountains is unpredictable. Even in summer, you might start a hike while it's sunny and finish it while it's snowing. Always dress in layers, wear good hiking shoes if you're hiking, check weather reports and be prepared for anything. If mountain biking, always bring a repair kit just in case.

Do consult our local Wildsmart.ca website for recent wildlife sightings in the area. ***Interesting fact:*** Banff and Canmore have an Elk population that numbers in the thousands. Be careful not to get too close, especially during their birthing season May/June or mating/rutting season September through October. Betcha didn't know that our average male elk can weigh 550 kg (1200 lbs) and have a rack that's a meter or 2-3 feet long!

Do carry bear spray. if heading out on a trail (bear spray is sold at most sporting goods and hardware stores in Banff and Canmore). Along with bear spray, remember to make lots of noise so you don't take a bear by surprise or get in-between a mom and her cubs.

Don't let your dog off leash. Leashes are mandatory everywhere in the Parks and Canmore area. Off leash dogs scare little people and totally annoy your fellow hikers and mountain bikers. Not to mention, our local carnivores find them very tasty! Please stoop and scoop as a courtesy to everyone using our trails.

Do go prepared to get hungry and thirsty. Remember that carrying water is a must. Always pack your food in and pack any leftovers or garbage out again to help keep our wilderness wild and pristine – just like you found it. Oh, and don't forget your hats and sunscreen as the sun up here is very intense. In our wetter May/June months taking along bug spray is also recommended.

Important disclaimer: The author cannot accept responsibility for any kind of inconvenience, self-inflicted injury, wild animal, feral animal, or party animal attack due to the use of this guide.

Beware of the Canmore bunnies...deceptively dangerous!

Using this Guide

Time estimate equation

$$T = \sum_{1}^{n} h * v * \frac{\sqrt{w}}{2s}$$

Roundtrip time estimations are very complicated. They have been provided in the Out'n About Day Tripper grid to give you a realistic time frame for each outing. In addition, the Day Tripper lets you know what you might see on each excursion. Each estimate includes the approximate roundtrip drive times (from Banff) and the estimated time it might take you to do the activity at a leisurely pace. I've documented whether the activity is easy, moderate or hard so you can map your activities to you and your party's physical ages and abilities.

Driving to our excursions are straightforward and we're fortunate not to worry much about traffic here. Even on long weekends and during the summer months trails are rarely too busy. After all, this is the Great White North, eh! Every excursion has detailed driving instructions so you don't get lost or divorced or break up because *he* won't ask for directions or *she* forgot the map. Free maps of the area are available at the Tourism information buildings in Banff and Canmore and most hotels in the area.

On many excursions "geocaches" can be found. We've always found it exciting to search for and find hidden geocache containers on our excursions and exchange treasures. It's cool to see who else from around the world has found them too and signed the log books. Geocaching is also a great hiking motivator for children so don't forget to carry small tokens or souvenirs to exchange in the geocache and bring your GPS device to discover them. You can find out which excursions might have geocaches at the up-to-date geocaching.com website before you go.

Note: Be aware that there is a mandatory Banff Park Pass fee. All cars entering with the purpose to stay and play in Banff National Park must buy a Park Pass that is visible hanging from the rear view mirror of your vehicle. Fees help pay our wonderful Park staff and help keep our Parks pristine and our towns wildlife habitat friendly. Fines are hefty if you get caught without one. Check the Parks Canada website for the latest National Park fee updates. As of this printing they run $19.60 Cdn for a family or group day pass. If you're planning to go in and out of the National Parks more often, a yearly pass may be your most economical choice. You can always sell your pass on ebay.com once you're back home again as there is always an after market for them.

"Pop"-o-meter (popularity meter)

Pop-o-meter

My mentor and the author of the guide book *Curious Gorge* – Scott Cook – has a similar rating for the excursions in his book (you must buy it if you go to Hood River Oregon or just to visit the Columbia River Gorge area). I've shamelessly borrowed Scott's idea. You'll see my popularity rating indicator rank excursions from low to high for each activity in my book. The sole purpose of this is to help two types of visitors. For you first time visitors, you will likely want to do the more popular activities. For those who come to our area more than once or are locals, I hope you'll also seek out the lower ranked excursions which are just as fun and totally awesome to try out too. It doesn't mean these activities aren't worthwhile. They are just a little less known but still great things to do. Some of them are things only us locals can tell you about.

my painting, *priceless*

Little Sister

Spray Lakes

Table of Contents

Inuksuk Trivia
A Few Notes from the Author
"Pop"- o - meter
Table of Contents
Day Tripper

1	Banff Gondolaaaaah	26	Montane Traverse
2	Bow River Hoodoos	27	Harvie Heights Loop
3	Bow River Float	28	Legacy Trail Bike Ride
4	Sundance Canyon/Marsh Loop	29	Spring Creek Float
5	Tunnel Mountain	30	Bow River Loop Trail
6	Billy Carver Pioneer Cabin	31	Bow River & 3 Sisters
7	C Level Cirque	32	Canmore Art Tour
8	Sunshine Meadows	33	The Highline Trail
9	Johnston Canyon	34	No. 1 Mine Trail
10	Silverton Falls	35	Quarry Lake Fun
11	Smith Lake "Zen" Hike	36	Dam Ruins Hideaway
12	Consolation Lake	37	Grassi Lakes Hike
13	Takakkaw Falls	38	Canmore Nordic Centre
14	Banff Honourable Mentions	39	Goat Creek Bike Trail
15	Barrier Lake Day	40	Ha Ling Peak
16	White Water Rafting	41	Old Goat Glacier
17	Heart Creek Trail	42	Westwind Pass
18	Secret Cave Hike	43	Chester Lake
19	Flowing Water Loop	44	Karst Spring
20	Many Springs Walk	45	Rainy Day Stuff
21	Brewsters Golf Ranch	46	Other Ideas
22	Mount Yamnuska	47	Events & Festivals
23	Grotto Canyon	48	Scenic Drives
24	Cougar Creek Day	49	I'm Hungry!
25	Lady Macdonald	50	Off the Beaten Path

II

Day Tripper

The Day Tripper grid is designed to help you decide on activities that meet your vacation interests and time limit constraints. Most guidebooks fail miserably at this. I've also tried to design it so you can pick stuff to do that is within everyone's abilities and age groups. It's not an easy task as everyone sets their own pace. Who knows how long a kid might want to dawdle to play and explore on a trail or a retiree will take to stop and read every interpretive sign and photograph every view. I've erred on the side of a faster versus slower paced outing, but it will at least give you a general frame of reference. As I mentioned earlier, I've not geared this book to the *Über* outdoors person. Easy stuff is really easy, moderate means you still can do it even if you're a weekend warrior and the hard category is bordering on *Über*, but not quite.

Each activity has it's corresponding activity number (not page number) beside it to point you to where it is in the book. Almost everything you'll do here will be scenic. I've highlighted excursions with waterfalls, flowers etc. to help you further decide your itinerary tailored to your interests. Hope you find it useful!

Moraine Lake

Day Tripper

Roundtrip Time Estimate from Banff (includes drive)

	Trail	Level of difficulty	Scenic	Waterfall	Flowers	Bike option	Swimming	Interpretive	Drive time from Banff (one way)
1 hr	No. 1 Mine Trail (34)	easy	•	•	•			•	20
	Bow River Hoodoos - drive (2)	easy	•					•	10
	Bow River Loop Trail (30)	easy	•			•			20
2 hr	Banff Gondola Only (1)	easy	•					•	10
	Sundance Canyon/Marsh Loop (4)	easy	•	•	•	•		•	10
	Flowing Water Loop (19)	easy	•		•			•	40
	Many Springs Walk (20)	easy	•		•			•	40
	Heart Creek Trail (17)	easy	•	•	•				30
	Secret Cave Hike (18)	moderate	•		•				30
	Billy Carver Pioneer Cabin (6)	easy	•		•		•	•	15
	Tunnel Mountain (5)	easy	•		•			•	10
	Spring Creek Float (29)	easy	•						20
	Bow River & 3 Sisters (31)	moderate	•					•	20
	Bow River Float Guided Tour (3)	easy	•					•	10
	Banff Honourable Mentions (14)	easy	•					•	10
3 hr	Bow River Hoodoos - hike (2)	moderate	•			•		•	10
	Grassi Lakes (37)	moderate	•	•	•			•	20
	Silverton Falls (10)	easy	•	•					30
	Canmore Art Tour (32)	easy						•	20
	Johnston Canyon (9)	easy	•	•					30
	Harvie Heights Loop (27)	easy	•			•	•		20
	The Highline Trail (33)	moderate	•			•	•		20
	Grotto Canyon (23)	easy	•	•				•	30
	Montane Traverse (26)	moderate	•				•		20
	Canmore Nordic Centre (38)	easy - hard	•			•			25
	Dam Ruins Hideaway (36)	easy	•	•	•	•	•		25
	Smith Lake "Zen" Hike (11)	moderate	•			•			45
4 hr	Takakkaw Falls (13)	easy	•	•				•	60
	Westwind Pass (42)	moderate	•						45
	C Level Cirque (7)	moderate	•		•			•	15
	Legacy Trail (28)	moderate	•			•			10
	Cougar Creek Day (24)	easy	•			•	•		20
	Consolation Lake (12)	moderate	•		•				55
	White Water Rafting Tour (16)	easy	•				•	•	45
	Banff Gondola Hike Up option (1)	hard	•					•	10
	Sunshine Meadows (8)	moderate	•		•			•	20
	Mount Yamnuska (22)	mod	•		•				40
	Quarry Lake Fun (35)	easy	•				•		20
	Karst Spring (44)	easy	•	•	•				60
	Ha Ling Peak (40)	hard	•						30
5+ hr	Old Goat Glacier (41)	moderate	•	•	•				45
	Chester Lake (43)	moderate	•		•				50
	Bow River Float Self Guided (3)	moderate	•						15
	Barrier Lake Day (14)	easy	•			•	•		45
	Brewsters Golf Ranch (20)	easy	•						45
	Lady MacDonald (25)	hard	•			•		•	20
	Goat Creek Bike Trail (39)	moderate	•			•	•		30

1 BANFF GONDOL*AAAAAH*
Get up fast, take it in slowwww

Pop-o-meter
- Easy gondola ride or hike up
5.5 kms (3.4 mi) one-way, 700 m
(2,300 ft) elevation gain
- Restroom: yes
- Views and varmints

The Banff Gondola is easily one of the most popular activities to do when in Banff. Over half a million people every year hop on the gondola to ride up to the 2,281 m (7,486 ft) summit of Sulphur Mountain for the 360 degree views. Challenge yourself to do the unrelenting hike up the 29 switchbacks of the Sulphur Mountain trail and take the Gondola back down again. Or, do the easy round trip gondola ride. The views at the top on a clear day are wonderful. Definitely take the 20 minute stroll along the boardwalk that leads to the summit of Sanson Peak where a stone weather observatory was built back in 1903. If you hiked up Sulphur, you'll appreciate the fact that Norman Sanson the park meteorologist, hiked up this mountain over 1,000 times to record data at the observatory.

Potential up close and personal encounters with families of Bighorn Sheep who frequent the area are common. Beware the cheeky Whiskey Jack birds who'll try to land on your hand or picnic table to steal your snacks.

Compliments of Banff Photography

DRIVE: Once in Banff, head across the Bow River bridge and turn left at the lights. Keep right on Mountain Avenue following it up past the Rimrock Hotel to the Upper Hot Springs parking lot and Gondola base building.

Boardwalk with great views!

You might also enjoy the Banff Alpine Lights Mountain Top evening dining experience. Offered on Saturday nights at the Sulphur Mountain summit restaurant, you can indulge in a delicious Alberta beef prime rib dinner and treat your eyes to a spectacular scenic sunset and sparkling light displays from the surrounding mountains and the Banff townsite below.

Tunnel Mtn

2 BOW RIVER - HOODOOS
Cool geological formations, educational, fun

- Hike: easy Trail is 4.3 kms (2.7 mi) one-way.
- Elevation: 200m
- Restroom: yes
- might get wet

Pop-o-

What the Heck is a Hoodoo?

It's a strange word, for strangely shaped rock pillars.

Over thousands of years, rain, snowmelt and wind have scoured the glacial material that makes up the ridge you are standing on, creating deep and narrow gullies. These hoodoos were once partially protected from erosion by caps of sod or harder rock material, which acted like umbrellas for the pillars.

The origin of the word "hoodoo" is unclear, but we do know that these odd features have had a place in people's imaginations for thousands of years.

Who? I don't know, check it out

You can see other hoodoos in the Rocky Mountains, including the

What the heck is a Hoodoo? A freak of nature, I think they look like they belong on Luke Skywalker's' home planet Tatooine. Interesting trivia on the naming of Tatooine: George Lucas initially intended to name the planet Utapau, but eventually named it after the actual name of the film location in Tunisia, spelled Tataouine in French.... but I digress.

From the Surprise parking lot the trail dips down on a set of stairs and is well marked. Keep on the main trail following the orange arrow signs, skirting the Bow River. The trail will head through a meadow and then upwards (elev. gain about 200 meters or so) until you find yourself up at the Tunnel Mountain parking lot. Take in the interpretive sign about Tunnel Mountain and then follow the stairs leading down from the parking lot veering left following a metal pipe sticking out of the ground. The trail

> **DRIVE:** From Canmore head west on Hwy 1 to the first Banff exit. Continue into Banff driving along main street and hang a left onto Buffalo Street. Follow Buffalo to the "Surprise" parking lot (real name) and park there. From Banff – just find Buffalo Street and the "Surprise" parking lot and you're good to go. If you opt for a shorter excursion, head up the Tunnel Mountain Road (first right off the Trans-Canada Hwy Banff exit from Canmore – in Banff head up Tunnel Mountain Drive) and park at the Hoodoos parking lot.

continues on for another 5 minutes to the Hoodoos signs and trail parking lot. A paved interpretive trail leads to some fabulous 180 degree views of the Bow River valley and Mount Rundle range to the south. A stop for lunch

here is a great idea. If it's a hot day, everyone will enjoy taking off their shoes and dipping their feet into the cool clear water and soft sandy bottom along the Bow River on your way back. We stop at aptly dubbed "big rock beach" for a refreshing rest.

Note: I mentioned in the drive section that you can do a much shorter version of this excursion by simply driving up the Tunnel Mountain road and starting from the Hoodoos parking lot. The trail here is paved for

Banff Springs Hotel

Bow River

Tunnel Mountain

Big Rock

Little rocks

Cold water

18

those who need stroller or wheelchair accessibility or just an easy walk that will take about one hour in total. Make sure you read all the interpretive signs along this trail. They definitely enhance the experience and help you gain a much greater understanding of our wonderful area.

You might see some kayakers, canoeists or river rafters enjoying a float down the Bow along the trail – doesn't that look fun? That's why it is my next excursion recommendation.

3 BOW RIVER FLOAT
Class 1-2 fun, easy paddle or guided tour

Pop-o-meter

- Boat trip: easy 22 km (13.6 mi) one-way from Banff to Canmore.
- Restroom:"depends"
- Will get wet

Nothing can beat the scenic splendor of a Bow River float from Banff down to Canmore! If you're a fairly decent kayaker or canoeist and not scared of class I-II rapids, bring or rent your boat of choice and put in just below the Bow Falls in Banff. Or, let one of our many expert tour guide companies take you down. Either way, it's a must-do in my book.

> **DRIVE**: From Canmore, drive west along the Trans-Canada Hwy 1 and take the 2nd exit – Mt. Norquay Banff – into Banff. Head into town on Gopher St. and then Lynx St. and turn left at the stop sign onto Buffalo St. At the lights, turn right and cross the Bow River bridge, keeping left at the next set of lights onto Spray Road. Turn left on Rundle and follow staying right to the Bow Falls parking lot. If in Banff just ask for directions to the Bow Falls parking lot.

We've enjoyed many fabulous self-guided floats down the Bow River and I recommend to do the trip later in July or August, once the spring run off has dissipated and the river current is fairly mellow. If you can choose a hot sunny day for your adventure, so much the better. There are a multitude of places to put out for a picnic along the way and do take advantage of the great photo opportunities if you have a waterproof camera. One year a huge herd of Elk plunged into the river and swam across just ahead of us! I was so enamored I forgot to take the picture!

Biggest thing to be aware of are the "sweepers" or fallen fir trees that sometime hang low from the river bank edges jutting across the top of the river or are anchored floating in the river. Steer clear as getting caught in a sweeper isn't fun, especially if you're taking an inflatable boat or raft. If you lose or puncture your boat, you've got a long walk ahead of you.

Cascade Mountain

BBQ on board...yumm!

Of course, life jackets are mandatory and remember to bring enough water to keep well hydrated on your journey. Pack some snacks or stop to have a picnic to make a memorable day of it.

We put out in Canmore as going further down river isn't recommended due to some treacherous-fast currents, log jams and other hazards. Float past the trestle bridge in Canmore and continue under the next vehicle/pedestrian cement bridge. Immediately to your right is a boat ramp and put out there. We have a second car parked at the boat ramp parking lot or we arrange for a pick up.

Another option is to book a White Mountain Adventures shuttle service. They will drop you off at the Bow Falls and/or can take you back to Banff to collect your vehicle. (bikeandhikeshuttle.com, 403-760-4403).

4 SUNDANCE CANYON/MARSH LOOP
Easy hike, bike, long-boarding thrill ride optional

Pop-o-meter
- Easy walk, even better bike. (optional long board ride), very small elevation gain.
- Restroom: yes
- Waterfall, picnic areas, birds

Suitable for a walk, bike or horseback ride via the neighbouring tour guide horse stables, the paved 5 km one-way (3.1 mile) trail to the canyon and waterfall is very picturesque. Enjoy some wonderful views of the Bow River and surrounding mountain peaks before heading up to the canyon and waterfall. There is a picnic area at the base of the canyon waterfall or, you can wait and have a snack sitting on one of the many benches alongside the Bow River. If you choose to extend your excursion, I recommend taking the dirt/gravel Marsh Loop Trail. This will add another 2 km to the trip but it's well worth the effort.

zippity do dah!

To begin your trip, the paved trail starts at the far west side of the Cave and Basin parking lot and has a moderate elevation gain of 145 m (470 ft.) up to the canyon and waterfall. We've seen skilled skateboarders enjoying a longboard ride down from the canyon (a rad thing to do but wear the right safety gear and try this at a time when the trail is not busy).

DRIVE: From Canmore, take the Trans-Canada Hwy 1 west to the 2nd Mt. Norquay/Banff exit and head into Banff. At the stop sign, turn left onto Buffalo Street and then turn right at the lights onto Banff Ave. Just across the Bow River bridge, turn right onto Cave road and follow up to the Cave and Basin parking lot. If in Banff, just follow the signs to the Cave and Basin national historical site.

On the way back, watch for the signed Marsh Loop trail cut off to your left to enjoy more great views of the Bow River before heading back to the Cave and Basin parking lot. Also a popular trail for bird watchers.

Note: The Cave and Basin Historical site is not open this year. Renovations are slated for completion in the fall of 2013. If their parking lot is unavailable, park along the side of the road and follow the wide dirt trail that skirts the Cave and Basin parking lot and joins after the Cave and Basin onto the paved Sundance Canyon trail.

5 TUNNEL MOUNTAIN
Moderate hike in Banff, 360 views, flowers

Pop-o-meter
- Easy hike with stellar views, 240 m (790 ft) elevation gain
- 4.6 km (2.9 mi) round trip
- Restroom: no
- Views, flowers

Hiked year round, Tunnel Mountain is Banff's most popular summit.

This has been Banff's oldest and most popular hike for over 100 years. If King George VI and Queen Elizabeth II did it, so can you! Busy in the summer months, I recommend going early to avoid the crowds. This is also a good excursion to do in the early spring as the snow melts here fairly quickly in the season, although it can be muddy.

You'll start a slow and steady climb gaining 240 m (790 ft) that will reward you with wonderful 360 degree views at the top of the Bow Valley, Banff, the Banff Springs Hotel, Rundle Mountain and surrounding mountain ranges.

ex smoker

DRIVE: From Canmore, take the Trans-Canada Hwy 1 west and exit at the first exit to Banff. Head left into town and then turn left onto Wolf Street. Turn right on St. Julien Road and look for the Banff Centre overflow parking lot on the left – park here. If in Banff, just ask for directions to the well known Banff Centre for the Arts.

Mt. Rundle

Interesting facts: Tunnel Mountain got its name because an early plan in 1882 had the Canadian Pacific Railway blasting a 275 meter tunnel through this mountain....*NOT*. Who's crazy idea was that anyway!

First nations people aptly named Tunnel Mountain "Sleeping Buffalo" because it really does resemble a sleeping buffalo from the northeast-side views of the mountain. Which name do you prefer? Personally, I think we should have kept the mountains name as Sleeping Buffalo.

6 BILLY CARVER PIONEER CABIN
Easy and explorative walk to a pioneer's cabin

Pop-o-meter
- A bit of history and an old cabin to explore
- No elev. gain, 3.5 km (2.2 mi) loop
- Restroom: yes
- Views, flowers
- Picnic tables

This fun and easy explorative walk will lead to a little-known pioneer cabin that was built by an English immigrant Billy Carver back in 1910. He lived a hermit's life, living off the land and working periodically in the mines. His cabin remains still stand off the main trail. An "any season" excursion, this is a well-marked, minimal elevation walk. The walk itself takes about an hour in total. In May, the purple calypso orchids blanket the area in abundance. Watch for muskrats in the marshy areas too.

From the Johnson Lake parking lot, head down to the lake and read the three interpretive signs. Head across the bridge and go straight, following the trail up into the forest. A short easy climb will lead to the benchland overlooking the Bow Valley and an awesome view of Mt. Rundle to the south. Check out the Hoodoos

> **DRIVE:** From Canmore, drive west on the Trans-Canada Hwy 1 and take the first Banff exit. Turn right towards Lake Minnewanka and keep right following the signs to Johnson Lake. From Banff take Banff Avenue out of town and cross over the TransCanada Hwy. Follow the signs to Johnson Lake and park in the Johnson Lake parking lot.

below the ridge too.

Continue following the path east through the forest again – you'll walk across a power line meadow past a Wildlife Reserve sign – and then reenter the forest. The trail leads back down to Johnson Lake. Follow it up a small incline and continue along the lake for another 8 minutes or so. Watch closely for an abrupt path on your left immediately past two pine trees that stand on either side of the trail – the tree on the right has a large rectangular scab on it where the bark has been removed. Take this path that leads back into the forest, away from the lake. In just a few minutes you'll see the cabin and the interpretive sign on your right. When you're done exploring, head back along the trail to the lakeside trail and continue on westward to finish your loop back to the bridge and the Johnson Lake parking lot. On a hot day, I recommend taking advantage of the the beach to enjoy a swim (chilly but refreshing!) or just savour a picnic you've brought alongside Johnson Lake.

7 C LEVEL CIRQUE
Moderate hike, history, views galore

Pop-o-meter
- Moderate hike with stellar views, 8 km (4.8 mi) round trip
- 455 m (1,500 ft) elevation gain
- Restroom: yes
- Views, flowers, exploration, history

What's in the name? No, this hike wasn't named after a new Cirque du Soleil act. But it is French and stands for "a bowl-shaped valley eroded by glacial action." The trail is moderately steep as it climbs the eastern slope of Cascade Mountain. You'll come across some fenced off mining pits and can explore the ruins of the old Bankhead coal mining operations.

Watch for hoary marmots, pikas, ground squirrels and cute chipmunks en-route and especially when you reach the rocky base of the Cirque. In early summer, wild orchids, clematis and many colourful violets bloom along the trail. Expansive and stunning views of Lake Minnewanka and surrounding mountain ranges reward you at almost every turn. There is no glacier now but at the base of the Cirque, glacial lilies make a cheerful yellow display for you to admire while you rest at the top. Enjoy!

30

DRIVE: From Canmore, take the Trans-Canada Hwy 1 west and take the first exit for Banff. Turn right and follow the signs up to Lake Minnewanka for 3.5 km (2 mi). Take a left to the Upper Bankhead picnic area parking lot and park there. The trailhead starts at the southwest end of the parking lot.

8 SUNSHINE MEADOWS
One of the areas most beautiful hikes

Pop-o-meter
- Moderate hike with stellar views, 200 m elev. gain
- 12 km (7.4 mi) round trip
- Restroom: yes
- Fees: yes
- No dogs allowed

Ranked as one of the Banff areas most beautiful hikes, the Meadows are particularly colourful in midsummer when wild alpine flowers abound. But, my favourite time to go is in September when it's not as busy and the green pine trees mingle with the rich gold larch tree hues against a stunning blue sky and turquoise blue lakes. It's awe-inspiring!

This is pretty much a full day trip if you do the whole loop and side loop around Laris Lake. 12 km (7.4 mi) of well maintained trails are

32

> **DRIVE:** Head west from Canmore or Banff along the Trans-Canada Hwy. 1 Take the Sunshine Village ski area exit and follow up to the base of the Sunshine Gondola.
>
> **NOTE**: You must reserve your bus ride roundtrip tickets from the Sunshine ski area parking lot up to the Meadows trail head prior to going. Call 403-762-7889 to reserve. Bus typically departs hourly.

easy to navigate and interpretive signs dot the way. Slight elevation gain of 200 m but nothing too strenuous, so even younger ones can manage. Another "must-do" in my book. Have fun!

The continental divide is cool. Water flows either to the Atlantic or Pacific oceans from this very spot!

9 JOHNSTON CANYON
Our most beautiful canyon and waterfalls

- Easy hike with soaring canyon views, 135 m elev. gain
- 5.4 km (3.4 mi) round trip
- Restroom: yes
- All seasons option, restaurant, gift shop

Pop-o-meter

We've often taken visitors up the Johnston Canyon trail, simply because it is the areas best canyon and waterfall combination and not too hard a walk, even for the little ones. Super popular, I recommend going early in the day, preferably during the week to avoid the crowds. Hikeable all year 'round, you can't go wrong as the canyon offers a variety of beautiful landscapes and photo opportunities in any season. If you do go in the winter or early spring, it's a good idea to pick up some spiked cleats to slip on the bottom of your boots to avoid slipping as the trail can be icy.

The canyon got its name from a prospector who came to stake claims back in the 1880's. It became very popular once the first road out to Lake Louise was built in 1921. This led Parks Canada to construct catwalks, staircases, bridges and safety features that make the walk very enjoyable. The trail takes you past a lower set of falls but continue on to the upper falls as they are the ones to see. Two viewpoints let you take in the 30 m (100 ft) high cascading torrent. It forms a turquoise blue ice fall in the winter months.

DRIVE: From Canmore head west along the Trans-Canada Hwy 1 - same if heading out from Banff. Just past Banff, exit at the 1A Bow Valley Parkway and follow to Johnston Canyon. Watch for the trailhead parking lot on the right

If you're looking for a longer journey, there is an option at this point to continue on another 3 km (1.9 mi) to the Ink Pots. We've never done this but if you do, let me know what you think. If it's worthwhile, I'll put it in my next book!

And, if you like waterfalls, you might as well do the next excursion as it's right next door to this one.

10 SILVERTON FALLS
Beautiful falls, avoid the crowds

- Easy short walk to lovely waterfalls
- Scenic drive to trailhead
- Restroom: yes

Pop-o-meter

A great alternative to the often busy Johnston Canyon walk, Silverton Falls, the lesser known neighbour, cascades 50 m (164 ft) down into a bubbly creek that's fun to explore. An easy walk for young children or older folks, it's only a 1.4 km round trip with a short 50 m climb to the top of the falls viewpoint.

The trail follows the banks of Silverton Creek. It got the name from the mining town of Silver City that went bust in 1885. About 300 m up the trail is an abrupt left fork which takes you up to the top of the falls for a great view. Then, head backdown and follow the trail over logs and roots up to see the lower falls. It's not well maintained on this section but it's very charming and fun to explore. If you're up to doing one more activity that's nearby and you have the time, see either of the next two excursions.....

DRIVE: From Canmore head west along the Trans-Canada Hwy 1 - same if heading out from Banff. Just past Banff, exit at the 1A Bow Valley Parkway and follow past Johnston Canyon. Watch for the trailhead parking lot on the right just before Castle Junction (also trailhead parking for the longer and more challenging Rockbound Lake hike I need to check out for my next book).

11 SMITH LAKE "ZEN" HIKE
Serene, peaceful hike and lake, avoid the crowds

- Easy hike, 3.2 km (2 mi) roundtrip with a very moderate elevation gain/loss of 150 m
- Restroom: no
- Flowers, pristine lake

Pop-o-meter

We literally stumbled into this hike after doing Silverton Falls curious to see what it was like. If you prefer no crowds, this one's for you! Start your walk by crossing the bridge and keep right following the Twin Lakes trail. In 50 m (165 ft) go left, following signage to Smith Lake. Mainly a cool, green forested path, there are some pleasant sunny meadows to cross where a wide variety of wildflowers bloom in mid-July. Steve Jobs would even have approved.

__Interesting fact:__ This trail and lake are named after a reclusive hermit – Joe Smith – who is one of Banff Park's most famous hermits. Joe lived alone in nearby Silver City from 1884 to 1937. Some say his ghost still visits the lake he most loved. We loved it too Joe!

DRIVE: From Canmore and Banff, head west on the Trans-Canada Hwy 1. Exit at the Castle Junction/Hwy 93 exit and turn left onto Hwy 93 crossing over the TransCanada. Take in the awesome Castle Mountain view (pictured below). Trailhead parking lot is immediately on your left (it's also trailhead parking for a number of longer lake day hikes).

12 CONSOLATION LAKE
A Moraine Lake option to avoid the crowds

- Moderate hike, 6 km (4 mi) roundtrip with 65 m (215 ft) elevation gain
- Restroom: yes
- Restaurant, gift shop

Pop-o-meter

Ok, Moraine Lake is really amazing but yikes! All those people!! No worries. Just go to Consolation Lake instead and enjoy a scenic walk with way less traffic. *NOTE:* You must hike Consolation in groups of four or more as this is a popular area for bears to hang out in too. As it was just the three of us, we tagged along with another group – no one minds.

Start your trip by going left just past the public washrooms and walk down to the bridge that crosses over Moraine Creek. Walk through a massive rockslide that created Moraine Lake. Continue on into the lush, mossy green forested path enjoying the bubbly sounds of Babel Creek.

Kids and nimble adults will enjoy rock-hopping the rocks and large boulders surrounding Consolation Lake. Stop for a snack or lunch at the lakes edge to rest and enjoy the views of the glacial-capped peaks of Bident and Quardra Mountains to the south.

Interesting Fact: Mount Temple towers above the other peaks that make up the view back down the valley to the north.

DRIVE: From Canmore and/or Banff, take the Trans-Canada Hwy 1 west to the Lake Louise exit (about a 50 minute drive one-way). Go left following Lake Louise Drive from the Village to the junction with Moraine Lake Road. Go left on Moraine Lake Road for about 12 km (7.5 mi) to the Moraine Lake parking area.

It is the third highest mountain in the Banff National Park peaking at 3,544 m (11,630 ft).

If you'd like to extend the day and have sturdy footwear on, consider heading up to Upper Consolation Lake. Cross Babel Creek below Lower Consolation Lake over the log booms and follow a rugged, muddy trail along the lake's eastern shore. At the far end, climb over the rock debris that separates the two lakes. Allow about another hour to your trip. It's also worthwhile on the way back to take in the views and interpretive signs at Moraine Lake on the short rockslide trail loop.

13 TAKAKKAW FALLS
Go see the second highest waterfall in Canada

Pop-o-meter

- Easy walk on a short, well maintained trail to the base of the thundering falls
- Restroom: yes
- Exploration, fun

TAKAKKAW FALLS

WHEN YOU SAY "TAKAKKAW" YOU ARE SAYING "IT IS MAGNIFICENT" IN CREE. IT IS THE RIGHT NAME FOR THIS 254-METRE WATERFALL, ONE OF THE HIGHEST IN CANADA.

DALY GLACIER, 350m FROM THE BRINK, FEEDS THE FALLS. THE GLACIER, IN TURN, IS FED BY THE WAPUTIK ICEFIELD. SNOW FALLING ON THE ICEFIELD BECOMES MOVING ICE IN THE GLACIER, WHICH MELTS TO BECOME TAKAKKAW FALLS.

IN SUMMER, THE ROCK FACE ROARS WITH THE PLUNGING MOUNTAIN TORRENT. BUT IN AUTUMN, THE MELT IS SLOWED, AND BY WINTER, THE RAGING FALLS NARROWS TO RIBBON OF ICE AWAITING SUMMER TO SET FREE.

July flow

42

> **DRIVE:** From Canmore or Banff, head west up the Trans-Canada Hwy 1. Pass the Lake Louise turnoff at the 55 km mark, and continue driving on Hwy 1 for another 23 km (bypassing the Hwy 93 North turnoff 3 km past the Lake Louise turnoff). The highway will descend into a scenic valley where the road flattens out and there will be a well-signed turnoff on your right leading to Takakkaw Falls. Take that turnoff and follow it for another 16 km to the end of the road, where there's a large parking lot. The kids will enjoy the set of two steep switchbacks that will test the turn radius of the car or RV you're driving....yikes!

Nothing captures the shock'n awe of the Rocky Mountains like the tremendous thunder of Takakkaw Falls. Plunging from above at a height of 380 m (1,246 ft) with a 254 m (833 ft) free fall, Canada's second highest waterfall leaves every visitor humbled. Fed by the Daly Glacier above, Takakkaw Falls' flow is at its peak in July when glacial meltwater is running fast n' furious. *Note*: The Yoho Valley access road, located just east of Field, is closed during the winter season due to high-frequency avalanches, and opens June through October for the summer season.

The mostly paved nature trail from the car park to the falls base is very easy. It is about a 10-15 minute leisurely paced walk one-way as you enjoy the increasing waterfall and river views for the entire time. Of course, all this accessibility comes at a price as this is a very popular and busy attraction so go early or late in the day to avoid the crowds.

One of the many signs along the path says that the word "takakkaw" means "magnificent" in the Cree (an aboriginal nation in Canada) language. I think that is a rather appropriate adjective, don't you agree?

14 BANFF HONOURABLE MENTIONS

I couldn't overlook these popular Banff area signature outings in my book. I've experienced both and can vouch that they are fabulous.

Pop-o-meter

As we move on in the book to excursion ideas in and around the Canmore and Kananaskis areas, I felt compelled to add this honourable mention Banff chapter. See my "Rainy Day" chapter for more ideas in Banff too.

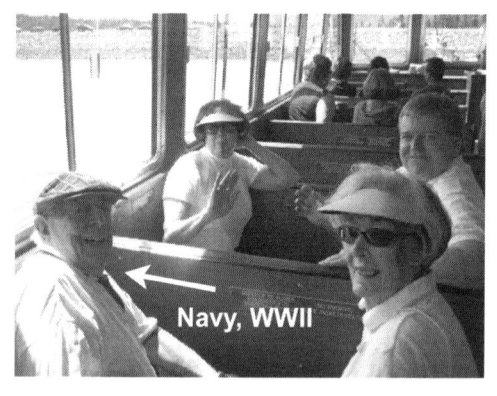

Lake Minnewanka Boat Tour

I took my visiting family on this tour and we all loved it. The tour guides are true comedians and we learned a lot about the rich history of the lake and it's inhabitants. Soaring mountain peaks and Lake Minnewanka and mountain scenery abound at every turn. This is an activity that all family members can enjoy. As of this printing, tickets were $45 for 16+ yrs, $20 6-15 yrs and kids under 5 are free! Open early May through early October. Check out the explorerockies.com website to reserve your seats. (recommended).

Upper Banff Hot Springs Soak

After all your outdoor adventures, a soak in the famous *au natural* Banff Hot Springs will certainly cap off a great day and sooth any aches and pains. We prefer going when it's cold, rainy or snowy. It's less busy then too! See the hotsprings.ca website for fees and hours of operation.

Free foot soak here

15 BARRIER LAKE DAY
Lovely walk, then a fun day at the beach

- Easy walk on well maintained trail to a Barrier Lake lookout + a beach day
- Restroom: yes
- Picnic, swim, boat ramp

Pop-o-meter

Interesting fact: This area was first cleared by German prisoners-of-war in the summer of 1945.

I recommend making a day trip out of this excursion to enjoy the brilliant turquoise blue Barrier Lake, the expansive soft sandy beach and picnicking area on a sunny hot day. The Barrier Lake lookout walk is an easy 2 km (1.2 mi) round trip up to a great lookout point. From the parking lot you'll see the interpretive trail sign that's perched at the top of a small set of wooden stairs. Head up the well marked trail as it switchbacks easily towards the lookout. Wild flowers, juniper and kinnikinnick add vibrant colour to your adventure in the late spring/early summer. When you've

> **DRIVE**: From Banff and/or Canmore take the Trans-Canada Hwy 1 east to the Hwy 40 south Kananaskis turnoff. Set odometer to 0 and drive 11 km (6.8 mi) south past the first Barrier Lake Dam exit to the second Barrier Lake Picnic/boat ramp exit on your right. Follow the paved road keeping straight at the junction and drive up the little hill to the parking lot.

finished the walk, drive down to the Barrier Lake day use picnic/BBQ area and boat launch parking lot. Raft, canoe or kayak, it is a stunning lake to paddle around too.

On the way home, it's fun to stop at the "Widow Maker" whitewater kayak course on the Kananaskis River to watch the kayakers navigate class three rapids. Take the "Widow Maker" exit on the left, just north of Barrier Lake. Park and walk down the path to the river. There's a pleasant little walking trail along side it. Competitors come from around the world to perfect their skills and compete on this man-made designed whitewater course. You might decide to book a fun rafting trip on the river or try it on your own. See my next excursion for details on rafting tours.

16 WHITE WATER RAFTING
Class one to three.....WHEEEEEEE

Pop-o-meter

- A whole family excursion on the pristine, beautiful Kananaskis River
- Restroom: yes
- Water fights, funny guides, adventure

Water fight!

One

of the best excursions we can remember put 3 generations of family members into a few rafts to go down the Kananaskis River on a guided trip. We hopped on the tour bus from Canmore out to the river and then everyone squeezed into wet suits provided. OMG this was fun! The tour guides were fabulous and joked with us all the way down, telling funny stories and giving us thrills and chills over the class three rapid parts of the trip. Our youngest rafter was 5 years old which is the lower age limit FYI.

With wetsuits on, it really doesn't matter if the day is that warm. Your adrenaline kicks in and the wet suits provide plenty of warmth for the journey. We had tons of fun water fighting all the way down with other rafting boats as well as our own. Tours usually start at the end of May and go well into September. A number of tour operators provide this service including the Canadian Rockies Adventure Centre in Canmore, the Inside Out Experience group out of Seebe near Canmore, the Rainbow Riders Adventure Tour company out of the Rafter Six Ranch and the Chinook Rafting company out of Banff. All the tour companies offer refreshments and some provide meals or snacks at the end of your trip. In most cases transportation to and from Banff or Canmore is provided.

Other ideas: This is an ideal break-the-ice and bonding event for wedding party groups, corporate team building offsites, big birthday or anniversary celebrations or that special family reunion you're planning.

So, just do it. Get wet and wild and let me know how your trip went!

49

17 HEART CREEK TRAIL
Go up a cool creek, see a hidden waterfall

- Easy walk 4 km (2.5 mi) walk on well maintained trail to a hidden waterfall
- Restroom: yes
- Might get wet feet

Pop-o-meter

The Heart Creek waterfall hike is an easy 4 km (2.5 mi) return creekside walk for young and old alike that crisscrosses over the Heart Creek and ends at a pool canyon and a waterfall. Hikeable early spring to late fall.

The trail is well defined and starts just behind the trailhead information sign. We enjoy all the bridges to cross while the kids like rock hopping and exploring along the creekside trail and then wading over at the end through a small canyon to see the hidden cascading waterfall.

I lost my heart in Lac des Arcs

Interesting fact: Heart Creek got its name from "Heart Mountain" (above) because of its unique heart-shaped formation. The mountain was formed by "synclinal drag" which is a downward folding of the strata that creates a trough depression due to the erosion of softer rocks. Lots of synclinal mountains can be seen around the Bow Valley. See if you and your companions can spot more of these unique formations on your travels

> **DRIVE:** From Banff or Canmore take the Trans-Canada Hwy 1 east past Canmore to the "Lac Des Arcs" exit. Exit immediately right to the Heart Creek trailhead parking lot area. It's about a 10 minute drive one way from Canmore, 30 minutes from Banff.

around the area. To see the falls at the end, you must brave the cold water and wade knee deep up the creek canyon and around the corner of the rock cliff or, if fearless, try a much harder short, steep scramble up the right side of the cliff to catch a falls view from the top. If you still have energy, the short and secret cave hike on the next page might also be in order. Check it out!

18 SECRET CAVE HIKE
Bring the flashlights and have an adventure

- Easy 45 minute one way hike to hidden secret cave
- Restroom: yes
- Might get scared

Pop-o-meter

Bring your flashlights and cold war stories as the Heart Mountain Cave is a local secret that kids will love! Rumour has it the cave tunnels were blasted out by some eccentric fellow in the 1950's as a nuclear war fallout shelter...or perhaps it was blasted out by someone for safe document storage...or simply dug out by a very large prehistoric rat. But the kids seem to like the rat story the best! From the overflow parking lot head west

towards a "Bear Facts" interpretive sign. Follow the red and green Trans-Canada Trail signs across a washed out creek gully a short way up the trail. Make your way around the gully and carry on to a gravel service road. Stay left and continue 15 minutes or so until you come to a fork in the path – go left again. The trail then gradually switchbacks a few times ascending from here and soon levels off as you continue west to the cave entrance.

> **DRIVE**: From Banff or Canmore take Trans-Canada Hwy 1 east to the "Lac Des Arcs" exit. Exit immediately right to the Heart Creek trailhead parking lot area. Park in the right hand side overflow parking area.

The inside of the cave is cold and damp even in the summer so it's wise to bring a jacket to wear while you explore. The cave goes back about 30 meters and then splits into two side tunnels. Kids love to play in the cave so be sure you give them lots of time. Panoramic views of Lac des Arcs and the valley are available while you wait outside in the sunshine until everyone is finished exploring. Look for climbing purple clematis flowers in spring and early summer along this trail – a "perennial" favourite!

I see the light!

Lac des Arcs

19 FLOWING WATER LOOP
Take the family on an excellent adventure

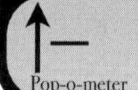

- Easy 3 km (1.9 mi) nature walk, minimal elevation gain
- Restroom: yes
- Might see a beaver

Pop-o-meter

With a variety of scenery to offer and diverse landscapes, this is one of our favourite self-guided family trails. Allow about 3 hours to ensure a leisurely 2 hour walk so you can take in all the educational interpretive signs along the way and visit the campground playground. The Loop trail begins behind this building to the right of the amphitheater trail. You'll skirt the Kananaskis

Junior rangers in training

River, cross a stream, explore ponds and wander along to a bench that provides some great views above the river. You flower lovers will see a variety of wild flowers late June and into July on this trail and bird watching or beaver dam findings are wonderful diversions. You may want to combine the "Many Springs" walk with the "Flowing Water" walk interspersed with a picnic for a full day of outdoor activities. There is a large playground and

> **DRIVE**: From Banff take Hwy 1 east to the 3rd Canmore exit and then head out on Hwy 1A east. Continue past Exshaw and then take a right (south) on the 1X Hwy turn off towards Bow Valley Provincial Park. Turn left into the Bow Valley Provincial Park "Willow Rock Campground" east entrance that's about 3 km down the road and drive past the check in station to the washroom/shower/laundry building and park here.

picnic area at the Willow Rock campground entrance the kids will also enjoy.

Finding a geocache!

Note:

Visiting families should take the time to see the Bow Valley Provincial Parks amphitheater nature shows that run on selected evenings all summer long. Entertaining, interactive and super funny, the Parks rangers and staff endeavour to teach audiences all about the flora, fauna, aboriginal and pioneering history of the area. Call the Parks interpretive program line for dates and times of the shows (403) 673-3663, ext. 220.

20 MANY SPRINGS WALK
Flowers + birds + frogs + water = fun

- Easy 1.6 km (1 mi) nature walk, no elevation gain
- Restroom: yes
- Might get wet

Pop-o-meter

Many Springs is a popular interpretive nature walk renown for it's abundant wild life and wild flowers. Bright orange wood lilies, red and orange Indian paintbrush, yellow lady slippers, orchids, purple asters, columbines and many more colourful flowers blanket the landscape June through August. Also a great hike for you bird and frog lovers. It'll take about 2 hours total to leave time for an hour or so hike, stopping to read interpretive signs and enjoy a relaxing stroll around the 1.6 km (1 mi) loop.

The springs are really a network of wetlands so bird watchers will enjoy listening to the trill of redwing blackbirds and sightings of other waterfowl species along the way. Keep a look out for springs that bubble up out of the mud along the waters edge as you walk along the trail.

When you've finished the Many Springs loop, another great side trip is to continue driving along the campground road west down

DRIVE: From Banff take Hwy 1 east and exit the Trans-Canada Highway 1 at the 3rd Canmore exit. Then head out on Hwy 1A east. Continue past Exshaw and take a right (south) on the 1X Hwy turn off towards Bow Valley Provincial Park. Turn right into the Bow Valley Provincial Park west side entrance and keep following the campground road, staying to the left. Watch for signs for the Many Springs trail leading to the small parking area.

to the Whitefish day use picnic area alongside the Bow River. You might decide to bring a picnic and enjoy a great view of Mt. Yamnuska and the Bow River while kids play at the water's edge. Keep an eye out for majestic osprey birds. Their large nests dot trees and are also built on top of many railway electricity poles along the Bow River.

See excursion 19 for information on the Bow Valley Provincial Parks interpretive theatre programs offered in their amphitheater all summer long.

Awww..can I keep him puhleeease?

Spring bubbling up through the sand

21 BREWSTERS GOLF RANCH
9 holes of family fun

Pop-o-meter

- Family friendly golf course and deals for the kids
- Restroom: yes
- Might get a hole in one

Mount Yamnuska

DRIVE: From Canmore take Highway 1A east. Continue past Exshaw and go right (south) on the 1X turn off towards Bow Valley Provincial Park. Turn right at the sign about 1 km down the road for the Brewster's Kananaskis Ranch Golf Resort. About a 30 minute drive.

There's no better deal for golfing with the family than at the Brewster's Kananaskis Ranch Golf Resort. They have a 9-hole, family package every summer where kids can play for free every Saturday and Sunday after 4 pm with each full paying adult. Enjoy some wonderful views of the Bow Valley and Mount Yamnuska (see next excursion) while you play. Call for a tee time (403-673-2700) or visit their website (kananaskisranchgolf.com) for details. Reasonable rental rates too.

Note: Insect repellent is a good idea to have on hand at all our golf areas early in the season.

22 MOUNT YAMNUSKA
Moderate hike with terrific views

- Moderately strenuous 7 km (4 mi) round trip hike, 533 m (1,748 ft) elevation gain
- Restroom: yes
- Great views, rock climbers delight

Pop-o-meter

Stop for lunch

Interesting facts: "Yamnuska" is a Stoney First Nations word that describes the dramatic flat-faced cliff that heralds the start of the Rocky Mountains. The Stoney's requested to have the Mountain renamed "Mount (John) Laurie" in 1961. John Laurie (1899-1959) was a great friend of the Stoney's. The following inscription appears on a large rock on the Stoney Reserve beneath the mountain: "A good friend to the Indians who taught them to preserve their culture and their treaty rights, and helped unite the nine tribes into the Indian Association of Alberta. His efforts improved the condition of the Indians, and created friendship, equality, and understanding between Alberta Indians and other citizens. Over the boundaries of colour and race swept the will of the Great Spirit."

This moderately strenuous hike is lovely in the late spring and summer, but is especially stunning in September when the sea of poplar trees cast a surreal golden glow above you and the fallen gold leaves blanket the forest floor. The trail is easy to follow and has a few switchbacks. It is a slow and steady climb so take some breaks if you're with little ones. Keep to

DRIVE: From Banff, head east on the Trans-Canada Hwy 1 and take the 3rd exit in Canmore to Highway 1A east. Go past the little town of Exshaw and continue past the Hwy 1X exit. Watch for the turnoff on the left for the Mount Yamnuska trail head parking lot.

y o u

left as you begin the final climb towards the mountain cliff. We stop to rest at the base of the cliff (pictured left) and have our lunch. The views from here are spectacular on a clear day.

23 GROTTO CANYON
One of our favourites - a "must-do"

- Easy 4.6 km (2.8 mi) walk, minimal elev. gain, all-seasons fun excursion
- Restroom: no
- Pictographs, waterfall, adventure

Pop-o-meter

Ahhh, Grotto Canyon! Easily our kids & visiting friends and family most favourite hike of all time. ***Interesting fact:*** You'll often see large herds of Rocky Mountain Bighorn Sheep along the 1A Highway on the side of the road almost any time of year (especially in the spring!)

Exploring the Hoodoos cave

This 4.6 km (2.8 mi) return walk boasts tons of nooks and crannies to explore. Rock-hop, and find a few ancient Indian pictographs painted in red ochre on the left side canyon wall about 2/3rds the way up. You'll even be rewarded with a waterfall. We've never tired of this all-seasons excursion as there are so many unique rock formations and scenery everywhere. Rock/ice climbers are also fun to stop and watch along the way. Once parked, follow the BayMag Service Road west past the BayMag plant and

DRIVE: From Banff head east on Hwy 1 and take the 3rd Canmore exit to Highway 1A east for 12 km. Just past Gap Lake look for the green "BayMag" 2 plant sign on your right. Turn left into the BayMag plant entrance but go straight up the gravel road and park at the fenced area you'll see just ahead of you.

Ok, where'd the kids go??

watch for the brown hiker trail sign on the right. Follow the arrow right through the forested path and then drop down into the rocky canyon. At the T-junction, you can climb along the right side of the canyon to explore the waterfall up close.

Continue on then to the left at the t-junction and follow the steep-walled canyon trail up into a small, protected and beautiful valley. Older kids will enjoy exploring the Hoodoos cave you'll find above the trail on the left in this valley but be warned – it's a steep scramble to the cave and they must be very careful on the way down! We always stop for a snack here (the trail doesn't really go much farther) and then head back the same way. A fabulous family outing at any time of year!

Winter ice, sled run fun

24 COUGAR CREEK DAY
Another of our favourites - a "must-do"

Pop-o-meter
- Easy 2 km walk, minimal elevation gain, all-seasons fun excursion
- Restroom: yes
- In-town adventure, might get wet

So you're right in Canmore but you soon feel as though you're in the middle of the wilderness shortly after you start your trek up the trail alongside Cougar Creek!

Kids will love to rock hop up and down the creek bed as you wind your way up about 2 km to where rock climbers scale the steep cliffs. Turn around and head back down the creek and if it's a hot day, remember to wear your bathing suits & bring towels to enjoy wading, splashing and cooling off in the Cougar Creek swimming pocket – a local favourite. You'll see a small waterfall flowing into a waist deep pool (there is a sitting bench above it on the west side of the trail). We've enjoyed many a summer's day sunbathing and braving the chilly but refreshing waterfall and pool. It's not deep and the

DRIVE: From downtown Canmore, take Benchlands Terrace Road up over the Trans-Canada Hwy 1 and follow up the hill to the fork in the road at the Eagle Terrace eagle statue. Keep right and the parking lot is the first left just behind the eagle statue.

kids will have fun building rock dams, stick racing and sliding down the smooth rocks along the little water fall. Afterward, enjoy refreshments and one of the nicest patio views of the Three Sisters in Canmore from the deck of the Iron Goat Pub restaurant. It is directly across the road from the Cougar Creek parking lot.

Note: I've also recommended other eating establishments in Canmore and Banff that we have frequented later in my book.

25 LADY MACDONALD
Challenge yourself for best views in Canmore

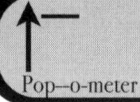

- Intermediate, fairly strenuous hike, 8 km (4.5 mi), 900 m (2,950 ft) elevation gain
- Restroom: yes
- In-town adventure, might get sore

Pop-o-meter

Go ahead and take the Lady Mac challenge. This is considered one of Canmore's signature hikes. It might take from 4 to 7 hours to complete it depending on how in shape you and others in your party are. Elevation gain is about 900 m or 2,950 feet in just 3.5 km or 2.1 mi. so I consider it "a

Canmore

strenuous" hike (for you weekend warriors). Round trip is 8 km or 4.5 mi.
Note: This is the busiest trailhead parking lot in Canmore so arrive early. Otherwise, there is parking on the road and in a small parking area to the right up Benchlands Trail beside the Eagle Terrace playground.

Start hiking up the left side of Cougar Creek. The Lady Mac trail forks to the left at the 1.0 km (0.6 mi) point. There is a trail sign to help guide you on your way. The steep and steady climb starts right away. Stay

> **DRIVE:** From downtown Canmore, take Benchlands Terrace Road up over the highway and follow it up the hill to the fork in the road where you'll go right at the Eagle Terrace eagle subdivision eagle statue. Parking lot is the first left after the fork, behind the eagle statue.

on the main trail – it is not signed but is easy to follow – and keep on climbing!

After a tricky rock section, you'll make your final ascent on the ridge that leads to a helipad and tea house ruins which is where most folks will stop to enjoy a break, explore the ruins and take in the scenery. To continue is very treacherous and exposed. You may encounter some furry and curious marmots along the way or even see some bighorn sheep who frequent the area.

Most people find hiking down Lady Mac is harder than the ascent so I recommend a pair of hiking poles to save your knees some stress. Sports Experts, Outside or the Valhalla Pure stores in Canmore usually have them in stock. Or, just find a sturdy hiking stick while on the trail. When you're done, pat yourselves on the back for doing the most challenging hike in this book. You've likely lost a few pounds too!

26 MONTANE TRAVERSE
Hike or bike the traverse

- Beginner to intermediate mtn bike, moderate hike on well maintained, fairly wide trail
- Restroom: yes
- In-town adventure

Pop-o-meter

Another convenient and fun Canmore activity is to hike or mountain bike around the Montane Traverse trail loop surrounding Silvertip golf resort.

To access the Montane trailhead walk or ride up the Cougar Creek trail from the Cougar Creek parking lot about 0.6 km. Watch for a trail sign where the trail forks left (look for the dead goat's leg hanging from a fir tree) and enter the forest. You'll ascend a steep hill. At the top, another sign will guide you to follow the trail due west for about 0.4 km. After skirting the Silvertip subdivision and golf course, there will be another steep hill with switchbacks to climb (bikers might want to walk/push here) to the top of the Montane Traverse. Then a really fun walk/ride across the top of Silvertip golf course ensues with some expansive mountain and Canmore valley

> **DRIVE:** From downtown Canmore, drive up Benchlands Trail and veer right at the Eagle Terrace Eagle subdivision eagle statue. Park immediately left at the Cougar Creek parking lot. Arrive early as weekends can be busy.

views along the way. If you are hiking, keep a look out for mountain bikers to allow them to pass easily. Keeping dogs leashed on this trail is mandatory and is important so bikers don't hit them. Once you've gone about 2.4 kms, the trail starts heading downhill and then forks off either right, straight or

left.

You'll want to take the narrow trail that heads back hard left or southeast which will take you right into the Silvertip golf course complex. Thirsty? Hungry? A stop here to enjoy Silvertip's Stoney's Grill patio for some excellent pub food and awesome views of the golf course and mountains is highly recommended. Or, keep walking or biking back along Silvertip Trail and Road east. At the end of Silvertip Road, cross over the paved golf cart path (you'll see a green trail sign). Retrace your steps east, keeping right on the trail, crossing over 3 fallen tree logs and staying right (south) back down the way you came up to the Cougar Creek trail and parking lot.

27 HARVIE HEIGHTS LOOP
Hike or bike the easy loop close to town

Pop-o-meter

- An easy mtn bike, or hike on well maintained, fairly wide trail, minimal elevation gain
- Restroom: no
- Close to Canmore all-season activity

The Meander, Montane, Tibits Quarry and Ridge Traverse trails combined offer a convenient, easy 7.2 km (4.5 mi) loop that everyone can enjoy as a family. A fun hike or mountain bike that is close to Canmore.

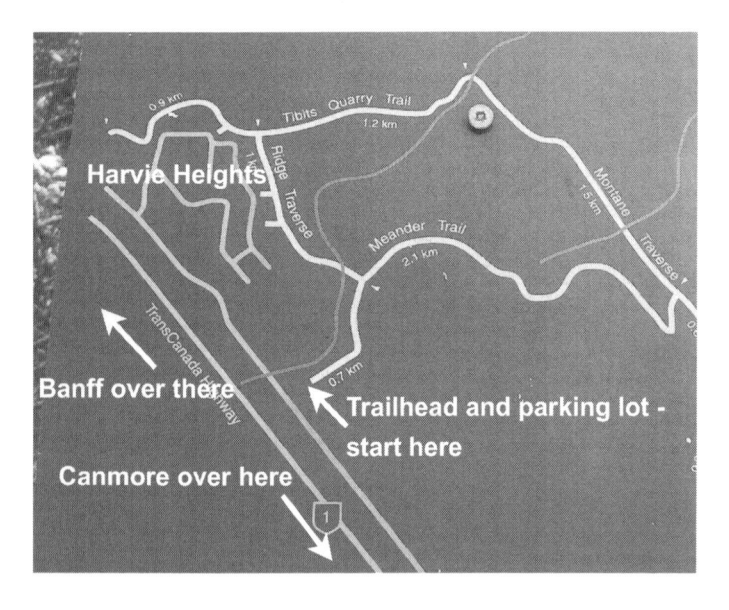

We've particularly liked to do this loop in the fall to enjoy the fresh snow-covered mountain views interlaced with the golden poplar trees framed against our brilliant blue skies. From downtown Canmore, it'll take about 2.5 hours to hike, less time to do a moderately easy mountain bike.

The trail starts just back from the trailhead sign. Follow it up a steep short incline and through the forest where the trail then splits at the Meander trail sign. You can either do the loop by going right along Meander Trail or left across the Ridge Traverse. All the trails are wide and well marked.

DRIVE: From downtown Canmore, take Benchlands Trail over the Trans Canada Highway. Go left at the lights and drive west on Palliser Trail. Follow Palliser Trail to the second Highway interchange and go right at the stop sign towards Harvie Heights for another kilometer. You'll see a gravel parking lot with a trailhead information sign on the right just before the hamlet of Harvie Heights. Park here.

As you head a bit higher, and cross the Montane Traverse section of the trail, peekaboo views across the valley of the Rundle Mountain range, and above you of Lady MacDonald and the north side mountain ranges are available.

28 BIKE THE LEGACY TRAIL
Paved, almost flat ride connects Banff to Canmore

Pop-o-meter
- An easy bike ride on a paved trail, minimal elevation gain/loss
- Restroom: yes
- Picnic, ride, all will enjoy a great day

The paved legacy trail between Banff and Canmore opened in July 2010 to commemorate Banff National Park's 100th anniversary. We absolutely love it! Faster riders can do the round trip 44 km (27 mi) in about 2.5 hours. Slower riders will take about 3 to 4 hours. Allow another hour or so if you stop to picnic at the Cascade Ponds near Banff or at the Valley View picnic area that is south of Trans-Canada Hwy 1 midway along the trail.

Cascade Ponds

Nice bike

Starting from Canmore

If you're biking from downtown Canmore take Benchlands Trail over the Trans-Canada highway. Go left at the lights onto Palliser Trail and down the hill past the Holiday Inn. Just across the Silvertip Trail road past the Holiday Inn hotel, ride on the paved path that borders the Palliser Trail road on the right. Continue past Harvie Heights and then cross over Palliser Trail riding on the left hand shoulder of the road and cross over the Hwy 1 Harvie Heights off-ramp. Continue on the Hwy 1 left shoulder for about 200 meters to the Legacy Trail gate marker path entrance you'll see directly across from the Banff Park Gates. ***Note:*** Some people opt to drive to the Banff Park gates with their bikes and park to the left before the gate entrance. Be very careful crossing the busy Trans-Canada Hwy to get on the trail.

Starting from Banff

Head out of town on Banff Avenue on the paved trail beside the road. The path dips down to a gated underpass. Go through the gates and continue on your ride. The Cascade Ponds parking lot is where you can start if driving with your bikes. The Legacy Trail starts at the east end of the Cascade Ponds parking lot and borders the smaller ponds before it dips under the Trans-Canada Highway to the Legacy Trail gated area. Head through the east (left side) gate and ride as far you want.

Be sure to stop for a rest at the Hwy 1 rest area also known as the

Valley View picnic area between Banff and Canmore. It's a welcome halfway spot to enjoy some sweeping valley and Mt. Rundle views from the

benchland edge. Picnic tables and washrooms are also available here for your pit stop.

Interesting fact:
The photo (below) is one of the "lock blocks" – concrete blocks that reinforce the sides of the trail. The artist – Francis – is a local fellow.

Imagine how fast he had to work on his drawing before the concrete hardened. See if you can spot it on your ride. There are more of Francis' artistic blocks to be found in and around Canmore too. It might be fun to make a game of it and find them all.

Hint: One is across the street from the Stonewaters store on main street in Canmore. Look for his initials "FS" on the block. Check for one too on the Marra's Way near Bella Crusta pizza again in downtown Canmore.

The Legacy is getting rather popular in the summer months so be sure to stay on the right side of the trail and make sure that members of your party ride single file at all times. Pass with care and, remember to smile and wave at everyone as you pass them by!

Don't have bikes? You can rent them at Gear Up sports rental store, Sports Experts or Trail Sports in Canmore. In Banff, a number of shops and outfitters will rent you bikes including The Ski Stop, and Banff Adventures Unlimited. As of this printing, your bike rental should range in price from $20 - $45 a day depending on what kind of bike you rent. Check with your hotel too as they may rent or have bikes to lend out to their guests.

Only want to bike one way? Lucky for you the White Mountain Adventures company will continue to offer a shuttle pick up service on either end of the Legacy Trail this year. Check out their pick up and drop off times and rates at their bikeandhikeshuttle.com website or call them at 403-760-4403.

Happy biking!

29 SPRING CREEK FLOAT
Fun and frivolous float through Canmore

Pop-o-meter

- Grab an inner tube, raft or a small kayak and enjoy an hours float through town
- Restroom: no
- Probably get wet feet

A little local bit of local Canmore fun! You must do the float in June through early July to take advantage of our winter snow melt run off that swells Policeman's Creek and Spring Creek to floatable levels. Even then, a bit of pushing or walking through the shallow bits might be necessary, but this just seems to add to the adventure. Helmets really aren't necessary as there are no rapids and the creek itself doesn't get much higher than knee deep except at few deeper spots along the Spring Creek portion of the float. However, I suppose you could bump your head as you go under the

DRIVE: You'll be putting your boats in at the culvert pictured below that's downtown on 8th Avenue, just south of 7th street. A large green bear-proof garbage bin is located just south of the culvert.

second vehicle bridge for main street depending on how high the creeks water level is – Doh!

You'll put out when you reach the end of the Spring Creek Mountain Village subdivision another 5 minutes or so past the third bridge. Arrange for a pick up there. The whole float will take about an hour.

30 BOW RIVER LOOP TRAIL
Beautiful, flat trail right in Canmore

Pop-o-meter

- An easy interpretive nature walk or bike ride on a well maintained gravel trail
- Restroom: yes
- Stroller and wheelchair friendly

This wheelchair, stroller and bike friendly path will be sure to please at any time of year with wonderful views and some great photo-ops. Conveniently located right in downtown Canmore, allow for about 2 hours if you want to explore the rivers edge along the way or grab a bike for a 45 minute ride. Have a picnic and let the kids wade and splash in the Bow River at Riverside Park if it's a hot summer day.

> **DRIVE:** The best place to park and start your walk is at Canmore's Millennium Park. At the Main Street Canmore set of lights, turn south onto 6th Avenue and follow keeping left as it skirts around Centennial Park. Continue south as it turns into 5th Avenue driving 4 blocks to where the road ends at the Millennium Park parking lot.

To access this 2.5 km (1.5 mi) round trip trail, begin by walking southwest past the Millennium Park sports field bleachers, through the mountain bike skills park and go right when you arrive at the gravel path that borders the Bow River. Follow the path, crossing under the pedestrian and car bridge, past Riverside Park and continue up the trail to the old railway trestle bridge. Take some photos here. Cross over the trestle bridge and walk past the little power plant. Head back down the other side of the Bow River.

After you've gone through the underpass, you'll want to keep right to cross back over the Bow River on the bridge. Then retrace your steps along the river trail right as you head back to your car at Millennium Park.

31 BOW RIVER & 3 SISTERS
Another Bow River beauty with some history too

- An easy interpretive nature walk or bike ride on a well maintained gravel/paved trail
- Restroom: no
- Stroller and wheelchair friendly

Pop-o-meter

Another fabulous path in Canmore that's stroller, wheelchair and bike friendly. A stop at the West Canmore playground is a fun diversion for younger children. Starting in town, it's about 2.75 hours to walk, 1.5 hours to bike it round trip. Allow for more time if the kids want to have some fun at the large playground or explore some of the mining history remnants along the way.

Follow the wide gravel trail right or southeast away from the Bow River bridge, skirting along the Bow River and through a fragrant wolf willow grove. The trail passes the West Canmore Park and playground and then crosses over a small creek bridge. It then ascends a short steep pitch before leveling off again. Watch closely for a fork in the trail in about 200 meters. Keep

> **DRIVE:** From Canmore's Main Street, head down 8th Avenue and cross over the Bow River bridge. Immediately left after the bridge is a gravel entrance to a small parking lot and boat ramp. Park here but arrive early as this can be a busy parking lot in the summer. More parking is available on the side streets around the boat ramp parking lot.

left, dipping down and up again to get back alongside the Bow River, passing some big homes. Keep left again onto the paved meadow path that curves around past two abandoned old mine shafts you can explore. Find the miners lamp house ruins to the left above them to check out as well.

As you continue on, you'll head up and then down a couple of switchbacks and enter the cool forest as the path skirts along the turquoise Bow River scenery. Keep left when the trail forks and go past the Cairns Landing subdivision. The trail will then switchback up a steep section. You can stop here or carry on across the Three Sisters Pkwy and follow the trail up into the Three Sisters subdivision. On a bike, explore around the area, maybe stop at the playground or The Market Bistro on Dyrgas Gate for a bite and admire the views before heading back the way you came.

32 CANMORE ART TOUR
Embrace your inner-artist

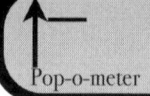

- Canmore boasts a plethora of talented artists and artisans who call our town home
- Restroom: yes
- Stroller and wheelchair friendly

Pop-o-meter

Take a leisurely stroll to check out some of our signature public art works and art galleries around town. I recommend to do this walkabout on a Saturday or Sunday to catch the "Art in the Park" shows as well.

Walkabout Directions:

Park your car in the large parking lot that's behind the Bank of Montreal on Main Street. Go to the Main Street stop lights and head right (east) up Main Street to the "Art in the Park" show at the little park beside the old Northwest Mounted Police Barracks. Members of the Canmore Artist and Artisan's Guild (CAAG) exhibit and sell their wonderful artworks here every weekend in the summer months.

When you're done, cross the road and check out *"Ceannmõre"* by Alan Henderson. This sculpture is made from blue granite and weighs 9.5 tons. The story lies behind the Celtic origins of Canmore's name. Malcolm of Canmore was an early Scottish King. 'Ceannmõre's' literal translation is 'big head', a reference to the leader. Malcolm is credited in Scottish history with the killing of MacBeth. Locals often make our big head a festive hat depending on the time of year. Continue walking down this side of Main Street, dropping in on Arty Farty and All in the Wild galleries. Then carry on down Main Street to check out the life-sized Miner's statue that stands beside the old Canmore Hotel that was built in 1888. Artist Lorne Wall created this life sized bronze statue of a miner as a tribute to all the men who worked in the Canmore coal mines. The mines closed here for good in July 1979 but we still honour them at our annual Miner's Day parade.

Follow Main Street down to 8th Avenue and go left. Head across the Bow River bridge and up the path on the left (east) that skirts the Bow River. *"Chinook"* is about 75 meters up the trail. The sculpture is made of fibre glass and steel. Standing 23 feet high Chinook represents the cycles of nature through the flow of a ribbon. Its abstract simplicity has attracted quite a bit of attention and intense discussion in town over the years.

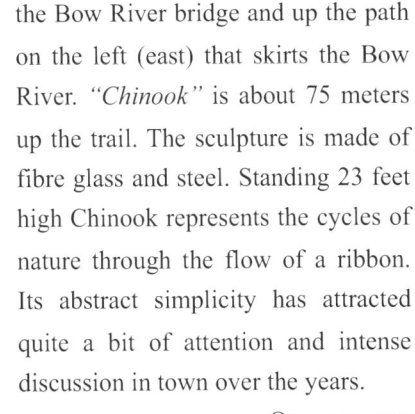

On your way back, visit the locals artist exhibits in the Canmore Library gallery behind "The Wood" restaurant on Main Street.

Finish off your tour by checking out all the Main Street galleries on the south side – The Avens, Elevation, and our newest addition, the Carter-Ryan gallery. That will cap off your art tour walkabout!

33 THE HIGHLINE TRAIL
An almost-new mountain bike/hiking trail

Pop-o-meter

- Intermediate mountain bike, easy to moderate hike near town (about 4.5 km (2.8 mi)
- Restroom: yes – at Quarry Lake swim park

A well-maintained trail designed for mountain bikers, hikers and puppies-in-training, the Highline offers fresh mountain air and some lovely views of Canmore, the valley and northern mountain ranges.

Puppy friendly!

Take the off leash dog walking trail directly south of the Quarry Lake/off-leash dog parking area and head across the open meadow towards the mountains. Re-leash dogs, and keep going through a forested area veering left. When you come to the power line trail, continue across it under the power lines to link up into the Highline Trail west connector – a large square yellow sign marks the trailhead. Follow trail up into the forest. A series of fairly steep switchbacks takes you 250 meters up the mountain to where the trail evens off and then you'll enjoy an easy traverse across the mountain. You'll get some panoramic views of Canmore, the valley and northern mountain ranges. After you go by the third dry creek bed, you'll start to descend the trail. At about the 4 km mark, you'll want to watch to take the Highline Trail east connector left and head back down the mountain

DRIVE: Drive west along Canmore's main street and turn left on 8th Avenue. Follow over the Bow River bridge and after a sharp right turn in the road turn left onto Three Sisters Drive. Just up the hill veer right onto the Spray Lakes Road. Look for the large gravel Quarry Lake/off leash dog park parking area on your left about 200 meters up the road. Park here.

Kids explore a dry creek bed

160 meters. (Bikers or stronger hikers may want to continue straight and do the whole Highline Trail that is 8 kms (5 mi) one-way into the Three Sisters subdivision.) Link back up to the Powerline trail, following it left and west back towards Quarry Lake. Look for the first fork in the trail as you get closer to Quarry Lake and head right. This will take you to the path around the shoreline of Quarry Lake and will lead you back to the Quarry Lake parking lot.

Canmore

34 NO.1 MINE TRAIL
Nifty nature walk with some history thrown in

- 1 hour walk for all ages, minimal elevation gain/loss
- Restroom: no
- May see a beaver

Pop-o-meter

A scenic, short walk complete with a little waterfall, mine ruins, views and potential beaver sightings. The No. 1 mine was the first of the Canmore areas many mines. It is situated in a pleasant ravine on the opposite bank of the Bow River from the townsite. No. 1 opened in 1887 and closed in 1916. Today what remains are the concrete walls of one of the surface buildings and coal seams galore. This is a fun little explorative walkabout.

Start your walk by crossing the Spray Lakes Road – the gravel trail goes left just below the road. Turn right after the big water pipe along the edge of the ravine and you'll soon reach a lovely little viewpoint with two benches that over look the waterfall and ravine. Continue on down the path enjoying the views across the valley and don't worry about the "Warning – Old mine workings in area" sign – they've all been filled in or fenced off. A long set of stairs arrives at a T-junction. Go right down some more stairs and past a large coal seam slope on your right and carry on to the waterfall for some souvenir picture opportunities.

Retrace your steps up the stairs and keep straight as you start to see the mine building foundation ruins on your left. Continue on the path, past a few houses and down to another little viewpoint and a memorial bench dedicated to Dr. Max Shafto. Who was Max? He was educated at the University of London (England) and graduated in 1941 in ophthalmology;

> **DRIVE:** Drive west along Canmore's main street and turn left on 8th Avenue. Follow over the Bow River bridge and after a sharp right turn in the road turn left on Three Sisters Drive. Just up the hill veer right onto the Spray Lakes Road. Look for the Quarry Lake parking area on your left about 200 meters up the road. Park here at the Quarry Lake parking lot

worked at the Calgary Foothills Hospital; was a professor and director of ophthalmology at University of Calgary; Died Oct. 21, 2001, aged 84. Max is survived by his wife, Jean who was one of our pioneering nurses in both Banff and Canmore.

Old foundations

Stop here and see if you can spot a beaver down in the creek below. You may have noted many of the poplar trees along the way are surrounded by chicken wire to keep beavers from taking them down. On your way back to your car see who can spot the beaver dam down in the ravine.

35 QUARRY LAKE FUN
Beach, BBQ and swimming fun on a hot day

Pop-o-meter
- Bring towels, beach chairs, picnic/BBQ, floaties, rafts, pails, shovels....but no dogs
- Restroom: yes
- Cliff jumping optional

Don't miss a summer trip to Canmore's Quarry Lake on a hot day! Take as long as you want. Bring a portable BBQ, have a picnic, swim, cliff jump, sunbathe and enjoy the views at this pristine and picturesque beach and lake. Once you're parked, grab all your gear and walk to the lake along the gravel path that's at the south east end of the parking area.

Note: No dogs are allowed.

Quarry Lake is quite popular now as the town of Canmore has added many improvements to expand the beach area and restroom facilities. Barbecues and picnic tables have been installed as well. If you

DRIVE: Drive west along Canmore's main street and turn left on 8th Avenue. Follow over the Bow River bridge and after a sharp right turn in the road turn left on Three Sisters Drive. Just up the hill veer right onto the Spray Lakes Road. Look for the Quarry Lake parking area on your left about 200 meters up the road.

Get a good running jump

Yipppeeee!

happen to arrive later in the day and the parking lot is full, folks are parking

A wild and crrrazy guy

along the south side of the Spray Lakes Road.

As you can tell from the pictures, one of our favourite activities at Quarry is cliff jumping. The kids and adults love it and it's not too high – maybe 16 feet – but high enough for the thrill. You'll see people jumping at the south east side of the lake. There usually is a rope swing to enjoy on the north side too where some trees hang out over the water. We've also noticed many wedding parties having their photos taken in the meadows around the lake, so if you're getting married, this is a great photo-op spot!

36 DAM RUINS HIDEAWAY
A secret spot to chill out at and explore

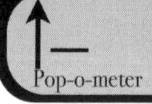

Pop-o-meter

- A fun secret little spot to enjoy a short walk to explore a waterfall and old dam ruins
- Restroom: no
- Might get wet, water guns optional

One of Canmore's little-known secret spots where you can enjoy exploring the dam ruins, picnicking to the sound of a small waterfall and sunbathing under the peek-a-boo views of the Three Sisters Mountains above you. On a hot day, everyone will want to play in the water pools so bring towels too.

Once parked, look for the temporary trail connection path on the right of the first gate. The trail will lead up to a second gate with a yellow and black sign on it. Carry on past this second gate and follow the path as it runs beside a lodge-pole pine fence. Where the fence ends, the path makes an abrupt right heading west and up into the forest towards the Three Sisters creek. Blue "Highline Trail" signs mark the way. Cross the creek bridge and

DRIVE: From downtown Canmore, take Hwy 1 east to the Three Sisters Blvd. exit. Exit the highway and turn right onto Three Sisters Blvd. At the four-way stop sign go straight. Head up the hill and park at the dead end just past the Hubman Landing Road. There might be some orange "No Trespassing Construction" signs but there isn't any construction going on as of this printing so don't let that deter you.

follow the trail keeping left after the bridge. Keep left staying on the wide trail, not where the Highline Trail forks right to begin it's narrow ascent. An easy walk for about 1 km along the creek and past a number of old wooden water pipes will lead you to the dam ruins.

Maximus Prime

37 GRASSI LAKES HIKE
Canmore's signature jewel hike

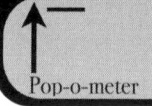

- A "must-do" hike for views, flowers, pristine ponds and pictographs
- Restroom: yes
- Geocache fun

Pop-o-meter

Fabulous waterfall, fabulous family

Canmore

A moderate hike with a total round trip of 3.8 km (2.4 mi) and an elevation gain of 250 m (820 ft), this is one of our prettiest trails so I consider it a "must do". Waterfalls, valley views, flowers, 10,000 year old pictographs, surreal, aqua-turquoise ponds are all yours to enjoy. Grassi Lakes was designated as one of Alberta's Special Places in 2000. The trail bears the name of its creator, Lawrence Grassi, who is a colourful, important figure in Canmore's hiking history. Mr. Grassi pioneered many of our area trails, and this was one of his favourites for obvious reasons. He lived from 1890–1980 and was an Italian miner who emigrated to Canada in 1912. After working with the CP Railway for several years he worked in the Canmore coal mines. A well-respected climbing guide as well as a builder of many trails in the area, a local school here also

DRIVE: Drive west along Canmore's main street and turn left on 8th Avenue. Follow over the Bow River bridge and after a sharp right turn in the road turn left on Three Sisters Drive. Just up the hill veer right onto the Spray Lakes Road and follow it as it curves around the reservoir. Just past the reservoir start to look left for the gravel road that leads down to the Grassi Lakes trail head. It is before the Spray Lakes road gate they use if the road is closed in winter for avalanche control.

Possible inventor of the hula-hoop

bears

his name. The Grassi trail starts behind the information sign in the parking lot. Make sure you take the path left where the sign reads "more difficult". It really isn't that difficult and the views and waterfall are definitely worth the slightly steeper climb – just take your time. The reward at the top of this hike will be two pristine, turquoise/emerald green ponds and just above them, some ancient pictograph paintings are nestled above in the rocky cliff trail. Kids love exploring the area and should also look for the hidden geocache so remember to check your GPS and bring a small treasure to exchange in the cache. While exploring, make sure to stay on the paths as erosion is an issue due to the trails popularity. Take the gravel access road at the left of the first pond for an easier walk down. There are two old cabins you can explore along the way back down this trail as well.

38 CANMORE NORDIC CENTRE
Canmore's 1988 Olympics pride 'n joy

Pop-o-meter

- An all-seasons recreation area, home to Canada's Nordic ski team
- Restroom: yes
- Restaurant, weddings, events

Developed for the 1988 Winter Olympic Game Nordic events, the Canmore Nordic Centre Provincial Park is a world-class all seasons recreational playground. Come and take advantage of the amazing trails and other first-class facilities. *Note:* Dogs are not allowed on the Nordic Centre trails.

Olympian in training

In the late spring, summer and early fall months, the Nordic Centre boasts an 18-hole Frisbee disc golf course, four orienteering courses, and has more than 100 km (62 mi) of single and double-track mountain bike and hiking trails, 6.5 km of paved rollerblade trails, and a mountain bike skills park to keep you busy. The best news is it's all **FREE!** The day lodge features a café, fireplace, changing rooms, showers, day lockers and rooms available for private

DRIVE: Drive west along Canmore's main street and turn left on 8th Avenue. Follow over the Bow River bridge and after a sharp right turn in the road turn left on Three Sisters Drive. Just up the hill veer right onto the Spray Lakes Road and follow it about 1 km. You'll see a big videotron sign for the Nordic centre and go right up to the abundant parking lots.

rental. Open 9:00 AM to 5:30 PM, daily but it's a good idea to check first to see if an event might be scheduled that could affect your visit as many world-class bike and ski racing events are hosted here all year-round. Even novice mountain bikers and x-country skiers will enjoy the myriad of well marked and maintained trails here. If you didn't bring your own mountain bikes, or skis, you can rent them from Trail Sports located right across from the Nordic Centre day lodge. A wide variety of sports equipment that won't break the bank ensures tons of fun for the whole family.

Note: winter x-country trail fees apply

39 GOAT CREEK BIKE TRAIL
Almost all downhill.....well almost

Pop-o-meter - 22 km (13.6 mi) from trailhead to the Banff Springs hotel, 45 km (28 mi) if riding back   - Restroom: yes

So worth the effort, this ride has it all. Wildlife, views, waterfalls and more views. Some parts are a tad steep but not for too long. This will be a full day trip – 22 km (13.6 mi) from the trailhead to Banff Springs, 45 km (28 mi) round trip if you decide to ride the "Legacy Trail" back to Canmore.

Mötley Crüe

The first 2/3rds of this wide gravel trail is mostly downhill so everyone will enjoy that part for sure! You'll appreciate your mountain bikes shocks as a few areas are quite rocky. A couple of creek bridges and a pleasant picnic area by the river make for a good place to stop for lunch. Continue on and up a couple of steeper climbs before ending with another fun ride downhill along the Spray river into the Banff Springs Hotel area. We've often stopped at the Banff Springs Hotel Waldhaus restaurant for refreshments, nachos and to enjoy their patio views of the golf course before biking back to Canmore on the Legacy Trail. A stop at the Banff "Bow Falls" is also worth taking in on your way back. Bring along a map of Banff or ask for directions as you

DRIVE: Same as going to Grassi Lakes (#37) but keep going up the Spray Lakes road, past the reservoir river at the top and then the road dips down to the Goat Creek trailhead parking lot on your right. Watch for families of Rocky Mountain sheep as you drive up this road - cute!

bike through town to get to the paved Legacy Trail that borders Hwy 1 back to Canmore. (#28)

Suggestion: White Mountain Adventures has a convenient hike and bike shuttle service to get you to the trailhead or pick you up on the other end. Call them at 403-760-4403 to find out the details: bikeandhikeshuttle.com

101

40 HA LING PEAK
Break out the hiking poles....you can do this

- Full day intermediate hike, 5.4 km (3.4 mi) round trip, 741 m (2400 ft) elevation gain
- Restroom: yes

Pop-o-meter

The second most strenuous hike in this book, Ha Ling will keep you in shape! Fabulous 360 degree views will greet you at the summit.

So, who was Ha Ling? Well, Ha Ling has one of our more storied histories in the region. During Canmore's coal-mining days in the 1880's, a Chinese cook named Ha Ling took a $50 bet saying he could summit the mountain, plant a flag visible from town and return down to his camp in under 12 hours (he left at 7 am and returned by noon!). The mountain was named Chinaman's Peak in his honour, though this wasn't made official until about a hundred years later. In 1997, due to the sensitivities of the name, it was changed to Ha Ling Peak, but not without opposition from those who believed the historical name should stand. Frankly, I like it that the name reflects the actual person it's named for, don't you?

Goat Creek valley views

DRIVE: Same as going to Grassi Lakes #37 but keep going up the Spray Lakes road, past the reservoir river at the top and then the road dips down to the Goat Creek trailhead parking lot on your right

Ha Ling trailhead starts across the road from Goat Creek parking lot – head north up the road to a gated service road, up a slope and then cross over a bridged canal. You'll then find a good path behind a shed and go from there. It is a steady and sometimes steep switchback climb all the way up so take your time (our seven year olds managed just fine with frequent rests and gummy bear treats). As you approach the summit, there is a challenging scramble crossing the steep scree. The kids did it on all fours in places and I was thankful for hiking poles, but it's worth the stellar views. *Note:* We thought we'd picked the perfect day once in July for this hike, but it snowed when we got to the summit and got very cold and *very* windy. Make sure you bring layers. I also recommend hiking poles to help save us older hip-hikers on the way back down – they are a true knee-saver!

Funny story: My in-laws were picnicking at the top of Ha Ling all by themselves when suddenly they heard a mysterious "voice" calling to them coming seemingly from the heavens above! Looking around they didn't see anyone but heard the voice say hello again. "Lo and behold" it was a rock climber just summiting over the north side of Ha Ling! Ya just never know who'll you'll meet on your adventures eh!

41 OLD GOAT GLACIER
Canmore's backyard glacier hike

- Full day moderate hike, 10.5 km (6.5 mi) round trip, 620 m (2,000 ft) elevation gain
- Restroom: no

Pop-o-meter

Want to know an amazing secret? Canmore has a glacier in her backyard! This is a true gem of a hike and well worth the climb to see a real live glacier before it all melts. Stellar views, wildlife, ancient sea creature fossils,

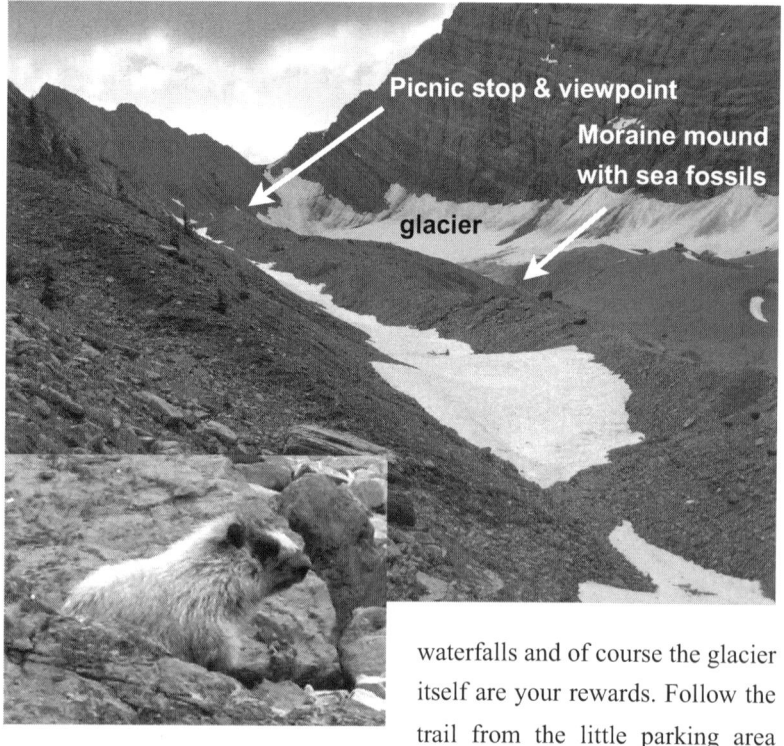

Picnic stop & viewpoint
Moraine mound with sea fossils
glacier

waterfalls and of course the glacier itself are your rewards. Follow the trail from the little parking area into the forest and along the creek's right bank. Keep bearing left on the main trail beside the pretty creek. About 20 minutes into the hike, you'll see the waterfall and ascent route – a series of steep switchbacks between a cliff at the left and a forest on the right. They are challenging but persevere to the top where the path then evens out taking you south-south-east to the

DRIVE: Same as going to Grassi Lakes #37 keep going up the steep Spray Lakes road, past the the Goat Creek trailhead parking lot at the top on your right and continue driving about 13 km (8 mi). Turn right at the sign for the Spray Lakes Provincial Park campground and proceed across the dam into the campground itself. Across from campsites #16 and 17 turn right into a small clearing where only a few cars can park. A sign indicates fires and camping are prohibited.

moraine mound path and views of the glacier and the sheer rock face of Old Goat Mountain. We stop and picnic at the end of the moraine mound and marvel at the glaciers force that carved this canyon. Marmots are all over the place up here but don't feed them! Look for ancient sea fossils in the large rocks scattered across the moraine mound.

Confucius says: It is never wise to walk on a glacier due to the hidden crevasse hazards and the unpredictability of melting glacier movements.

42 WESTWIND PASS
Easy hike and rewarding scenery

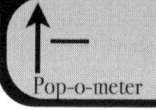

Pop-o-meter

- Moderate hike, 4.2 km (2.6 mi) round trip, 380 m (1299 ft) elevation gain
- Restroom: no

The Edge movie filmed over here

Spray Lake

The first few times we did this hike, we'd pay our respects at "Bob's Grave" where a small cross marker stood at the top. We assumed Bob had his ashes deposited on a rocky ledge overlooking Wind Valley below. The marker has been removed since, but we still pay homage to Bob as we sit at the top and have our picnic appreciating the fact that he had indeed picked a beautiful spot to be his final resting place.

Important note: This hike is closed April 1st through June 15th during the Bighorn Sheep lambing season.

The trail starts on the east side of the road across from the north edge of the pullout parking area. It initially ascends steeply but you'll be rewarded soon with some great views of the Goat Mountain range and Spray

> **DRIVE:** Starting in Canmore, head up past the Nordic Centre and set your odometer to 0. Carry on up the Spray Lakes Road (Hwy 742) for 18.5 km or 11.5 mi and park in the pullout on the right that's just before Spurling Creek.

Lakes behind you as you level off and traverse along the trail towards the West Wind pass terraced bench. Stop here to picnic, rest and take in the great views before heading back down the way you came.

43 CHESTER LAKE
Popular for a reason, flowers, views, larches etc.

- Moderate all seasons hike, 9 km (5.6 mi) round trip, 315 m (1,030 ft) elevation gain
- Restroom: yes
- Don't forget the camera

Pop-o-meter

If you're into flower power and want to tap into your inner-hippie, this hike is for you! The views at the top are also truly breathtaking making this one of the most popular hikes in Kananaskis country.

From the northeast corner of the parking lot, above the toilets and information kiosk, follow the former logging road northeast. You will pass a gate and soon a fork in the road. For Chester Lake head left/north on the broad gravel road and immediately cross a bridge over Chester Creek. Continue to bear left at all junctions as you ascend the road. After about 2 km, the trail leaves the wide road and heads left on a narrower trail into the woods. The trail will eventually level off into spacious meadows where flowers abound particularly in June and early July as glacier lilies and

> **DRIVE:** From downtown Canmore, head up to the Nordic Centre (#38) and then set your odometer to 0. Continue on up the Spray Lakes/Smith Dorrien Road (Hwy 742) for another 41 km or 25 mi. Just past Mud Lake and the Burstall day use area, you'll see the large Chester Lake trailhead parking lot on your left. This is a popular hike so arriving early is always best.

buttercups create a vast golden carpet display. Once across the meadows, you'll be rewarded by Chester Lake. Have a picnic and enjoy the scenery. Worth visiting in the fall season to ogle at the larch trees in all their golden splendor.

Although a conifer, the larch is a deciduous tree and loses its "leaves" (they look like little pine needles) in the fall. The needles turn to a rich gold colour by mid-September before they fall off the trees forming a lovely contrast to the green and blue landscape. Larches are unique too in winter, as they keep many brown seed cones on their branches. If you're back visiting us in the winter, Chester is a popular snowshoe, x-country ski or winter hiking excursion.

44 KARST SPRING
Great hike for you, Dorothy, and Toto too

Pod-o-meter
- Easy hike that's 10 km (6.2 mi) round trip and minimal elevation gain/loss
- Restroom: yes
- Might see Moose

The Karst Spring hike is really cool! Bog orchids, white paintbrush and many other eye catching flowers offer a bright contrast as you walk along this emerald green trail. At the trails end, water thunders out of a sheer rock face seemingly from nowhere and rushes down a rocky creek bed. Even the Wizard of Oz would be impressed.

Who let the moose out?

Look for the trail called "Watridge Lake" that starts from the information board at the entrance of the parking lot. Follow it to the old Watridge logging road past the

Overlook point

110

DRIVE: From Canmore follow the signs to the Canmore Nordic Centre, and stay on the Spray Lakes Road, which becomes the Smith Dorrien - Spray Trail (Hwy #742) for about 37 km south along the Spray Lake, to the sign for the Mount Shark ski trails road turnoff. Turn right and follow the road past Mt. Engadine Lodge (look for moose here) for another 5 km or so until you get to the large Mount Shark parking lot.

gate. Stay on the main logging road trail which will dip down to a bridge that crosses over a creek. Carry on the road trail and continue until there is a sharp left heading down to Watridge Creek and Lake. Backtrack a few meters and turn right to find the signed trail to Karst Springs. Follow the trail over a lush, marshy boardwalk area and south into the emerald green, moss-laden forest. You'll skirt the creek all the way up to a moderate climb that ends at the falls of the thundering Karst Spring. Sit at the overlook, ogle and enjoy!

45 RAINY DAY STUFF
Weather sucks? No worries...

Who doesn't get a few less than stellar days while on vacation? Don't panic, there's plenty to keep you occupied in Canmore and Banff until sunny days come back again. Fee's may apply.

Canmore NWMP Barracks

At the corner of Main Street (8th Ave) and Spring Creek Drive, this was Canmore's first police station built in 1893. Canmore's Mounties lived, worked and even housed their wild west prisoners here as settlers began to pour in. Bullet holes and many legendary stories from the staff will keep you entertained while looking at all the artifacts. An added bonus, they often have special crafts and scavenger hunts for the kids! You may even land a photo-op with a real live Mountie!

Friendly Mountie

Canmore Museum and Geoscience Centre

902 - 7th Avenue

This quaint little museum is located downtown inside the Canmore Civic Centre. Could keep you busy for a couple of hours learning about our proud mining, railway and pioneering past.

Canmore Recreation Centre Pool

1900 - 8th Avenue

Call first for public swim times - 403-678-1537. Children of all ages will have lots of fun playing with floaties, rafts and a rope swing that will keep them busy for a few hours at least. Adults can chill while relaxing in the large hot tub and watching the kids swim. *Note*: Stay tuned for the much anticipated Canmore Multiplex recreation facility slated for completion in the fall of 2012. This $40 million dollar facility will have a world-class pool, water slides, lazy river, climbing wall, fitness centre, host our new library and local artists art gallery. We can't wait!

Banff Lux Cinema

229 Bear Street, Banff

Take in an afternoon or evening movie in Banff. A great way to spend a rainy day catching that epic new blockbuster.

Douglas Fir Resort Pool and Water-Slides

At the top of Tunnel Mountain Road in Banff, they have two long 2-story high water-slides, a pool and a hot tub that will keep families very happy on a cold wet day. Great for birthday parties too. And, you don't need to be a guest at the hotel to enjoy this activity.

Canmore or Banff Shop 'till You Drop

Browse all the unique and funky shops and galleries along Main Streets in either Banff or Canmore. See my "Off the Beaten Path" chapter as well.

Banff Park Museum

91 Banff Avenue, Banff
Like stuffed animals? (taxidermy I mean) Well this is the place for you! Along with a treasure trove of historical and educational facts about all the wildlife that lives in the region, you'll learn a ton about our National Park efforts to conserve their habitats.

Buffalo Nations Museum

1 Birch Avenue, Banff
A first class look at the history and culture of our First Nations peoples. Afterwards, be sure to stop at the...

... Banff Indian Trading Post...

...right next door. This family owned business has been an icon of Banff since 1903. They have a huge inventory beautiful native crafts from First Nations bands all across Canada. Handcrafted aboriginal clothing, moccasins, jewelry,

Merman mummy

sculptures and accessories are truly a part of our First Nations culture you will want to take home. *Note:* Don't miss the weird and scary "Merman" mummy dude on display in a glass case in the back room. Our kids favourite thing to see!

The Whyte Museum in Banff

111 Bear St. The Whyte Museum has been under a major revitalization renovation, that was completed in May 2012. It was founded by Catharine Robb and Peter Whyte who met at the Boston Museum School of Fine Art in 1927. She was a beautiful Boston debutante. He was a rugged, handsome member of one of Banff's pioneer families. They married in 1930, and made Banff their home – *how romantic is that!* A studio was built one year later where they would live and paint the grandeur of their beloved Rocky Mountains. The museum now houses a large variety of fine art, photography and historical pioneer and aboriginal artifacts from the area.

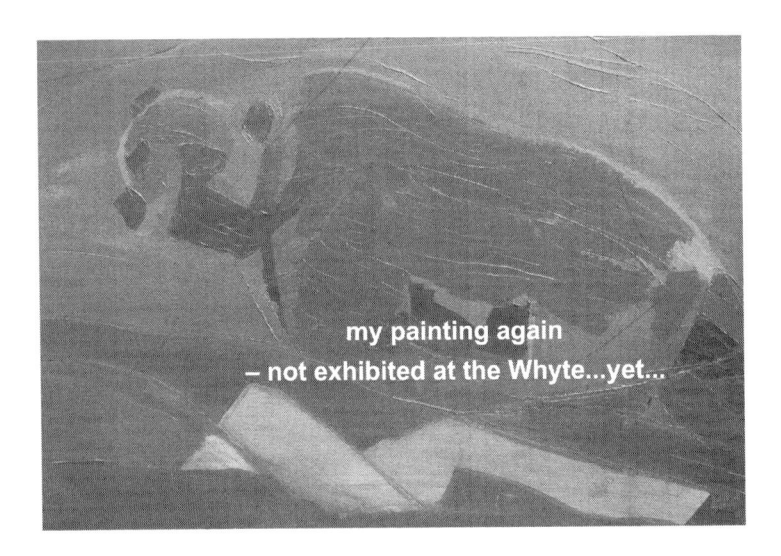

my painting again
– not exhibited at the Whyte...yet...

Banff Springs Hotel Day

405 Spray Avenue, Banff. Visit the historical Banff Springs Hotel that was built in 1888. On a gloomy day it's fun to explore the hotels nooks and crannies and, if you dare, seek out the **ghosts** that reportedly haunt the hotel! Then, enjoy a round of 5-pin bowling. They have 4 lanes but be sure to call ahead and reserve your time before going, 403-762-6892. Or, relax and enjoy their renown and authentically British, elegant afternoon tea.

So, is the Banff Springs haunted you ask? Well, legends tell of the most famous ghost – that of Sam McCauley. Sam was a Scotsman who arrived at the hotel in the 1930's to work as a porter for 40 years. Some say he's there still as he told everyone he planned to haunt the hotel upon his death. Guests regularly mention seeing lights outside their windows, well above ground level. Once a couple checked in late in the evening, and the next day asked who the old man was who

Don't trip here...

...or here!

helped them with their bags. The hotel employee assured them there were no bell hops over the age of 30 at the Banff Springs but the couple were insistent and described the man who looked like Sam – but Sam had been dead for two years! Sam's favourite haunt – the 9th floor corridor. Other ghost sightings include the Rob Roy Lounge that hosts a headless bagpiper and a long-deceased bartender who takes it upon himself to inform patrons when they have had enough to drink.

And, breaking news! Banff Photography now has proof! One of their female photographers was preparing for a group photo lesson on August 9, 2011 and took the private elevator which runs between the 9th and 12th floors to capture a few landscape photos. She took several photos from inside the elevator to show how to capture landscapes through window glass and several outdoor photos as well. Upon reviewing the photos she noticed that there was an odd reflection in the window of one of her pictures. It appears that there is a woman in the photo wearing a white dress with her hands at her side. The photographer was alone with her hands up at eye level taking the picture. There is a tale of a bride who tripped down the stairs on her wedding day, breaking her neck and wanders the hotel still, looking for her groom. Could the photographer have captured the brides image in the reflection? We will let you be the judge!

46 OTHER IDEAS
So much to do....so little time....

The author has enjoyed most of following excursions and can highly recommend them as additional highlights to your vacation.

Giddyup Horseback Rides

Book an authentic wild wild west experience! All our tours boast well-trained staff, and very user friendly horses. In most cases wagon rides, BBQ cook outs, western restaurants and authentic old west surroundings add to help make your day truly memorable.

Horse back ride trips are offered down Highway 40 in Kananaskis Village by the Boundary Ranch group. Closer still to Canmore and Banff are the Rafter Six Ranch and the Inside Out Experience folks. In Banff you can choose from excursions offered by the Holiday on Horseback tour company or the Brewster Adventures group. Right in Canmore, the Cross Zee Ranch is conveniently located just on the north side of town before you reach Harvie Heights.

Royal Tyrrell Museum in Drumheller Alberta

Yabba dabba doooo!! Drumheller Alberta is just about a two hour drive from Canmore or Banff and it is so worth it. This expansive display of fully assembled dinosaur skeletons and life-sized sized dinosaur exhibits will amaze and humble you.

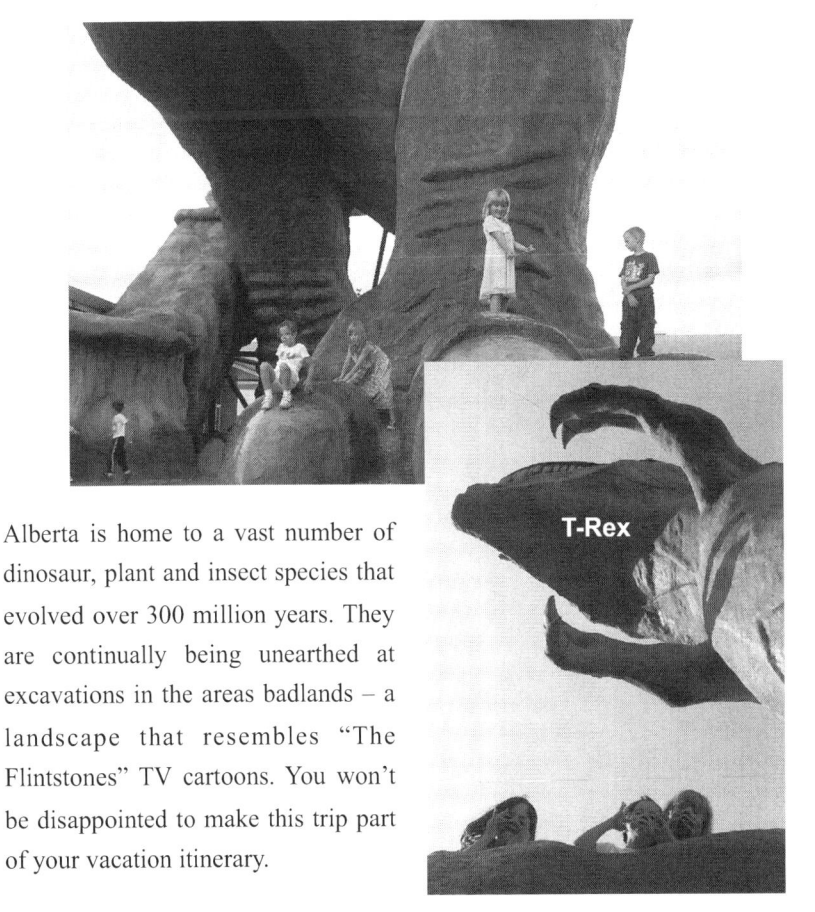

Alberta is home to a vast number of dinosaur, plant and insect species that evolved over 300 million years. They are continually being unearthed at excavations in the areas badlands – a landscape that resembles "The Flintstones" TV cartoons. You won't be disappointed to make this trip part of your vacation itinerary.

T-Rex

119

Calaway Theme Park

About a 60 minute drive from Canmore or Banff, Calaway Park is like a "mini me" Disneyland. This clean and quaint little theme park will keep the everyone busy for a day and is a great stopover if heading to or from Calgary during your stay.

Calgary Stampede!

If you plan to visit us in early July, another great activity is to spend a day or two in Calgary at our signature and historic

Don't fall off the wagon!

"Calgary Stampede", the greatest show on earth. A wild west extravaganza, the Stampede is going to be celebrating their 100th anniversary this year (2012). A *huge* parade, world renown chuck wagon races, rodeo competitions, country & western music concerts featuring superstar performers such as Kenny Chesney, Brad Paisley or Garth Brooks, stacks of fluffy western pancakes, barbecues, First Nations fanfare and an amusement theme park with all the fix'ins await. *Yeeehaww!*

"A River Runs Through It" Fly Fishing Experience

Providing excellence in guiding and instruction on the waters of the Canadian Rockies since 1985, Mountain Fly-Fishers offers guiding and instruction on the waters of the Upper Bow River and the Headwater streams of the Bow Crow Forest preserve. Go with my friend John or one of his expert guides and get the most out of your "*A River Runs Through It*" day. Base operations are located at Nakoda Lodge on Hector Lake (on Hwy 1A about a 30 minute drive east from Canmore). Accommodation packages including meals can also be arranged. mountainflyfishers.com

Paintball Adventure

Want a high adrenaline alternative to add to your Canmore experiences? Look no further than Mountain Paintball also operated at Nakoda Lodge. Although the minimum age for game play is 12, Mountain Paintball hasn't overlooked the younger folk who might want to have some paintball fun as well. They offer a shooting range where kids can shoot with no worries about getting hit. Check them out for more information at unlimitedcanmoreadventures.com.

"Fore" You Golfers

There is something truly unique and inspiring about golfing while enjoying our spectacular Rocky Mountain scenery, even if you really suck at golf. Options nearby include:

Silvertip Golf Resort $$$$, 403-678-1600

Stuart Creek Golf & Country Club $$$$, 403-609-6099

Canmore Golf & Curling Club $$, 403-678-5959

Brewsters Kananaskis Ranch Golf Resort $$, 403-673-2700

Kananaskis Country Golf Course $$$, 877-591-2525

The Historic Fairmont Banff Springs Golf Resort $$$$, 403-762-6801

Remember, insect repellant is a good companion early in the season. Keep a camera handy for close encounters with neighbouring wildlife and amazing views too.

Banff Photography Group Lessons

Banff Photography offers lessons and photo classes from their location in the retail level of the Banff Springs Hotel. Their photographers are keen on sharing their knowledge and know how, offering photography classes from basic to expert for both digital and yes, film cameras and techniques! Learn how to use your camera better, how to use new and exciting tools that are on the market today from flashes, diffusers, filters, lenses and tripods. You need to learn how to compose and take better pictures, don't you? I know I do. Check out banffphotography.com for details.

Canmore or Kananaskis Helicopter Tours

photo courtesy of Noel Rogers

A "bucket list" must-do. Alpine Helicopters in Canmore offers a variety of excursions and even offers groups and weddings deals. Imagine getting hitched at the top of a mountain! Surely you can find a reason to do this, once in a lifetime experience. alpinehelicopters.com for details.

Or, you can also contact the Kananaskis Heli Tour company that operates out of the Stoney Mountain Resort and Casino 30 minutes west of Canmore just off the Trans-Canada Hwy 1 at exit #40.

47 EVENTS & FESTIVALS
Music, magic, men in kilts...

Plan you trip around some of these local annual events to enhance your wonderful stay. Check the local papers too when you're here.

ArtsPeak - June

Canmore's signature arts festival boasts hundreds of local and regional artists and artisans who come to sell their wears. *artspeakcanmore.com*

Canada Day Festivities Eh!

Banff and Canmore both host our fabulous Canada Day parades, fireworks, music and fanfare every July 1st. Join in the fun to help us celebrate all things that are Canadian *eh*! Free events include pancake breakfasts, the wonderful parades, live concerts, games and activities for the kids and of course, an amazing fireworks display at the end of the evening.

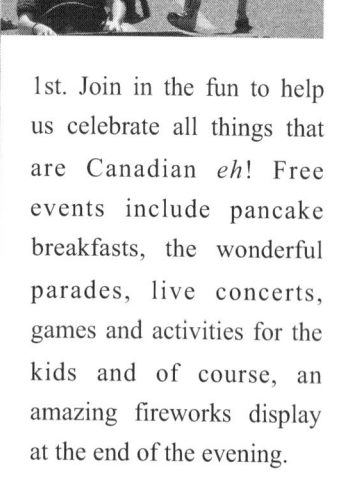

Hint: Put your lawn chairs out along the

Canmore parade route street sidewalks early in the morning so you can watch the parade in comfort. Kids will love scrambling after the parade floats to collect all the candies and treats they throw into the crowds. Watch out. You might also get wet!!

24 Hours of Adrenaline - July

Mountain bike mania! Over 1,500 men and women congregate from around the world to compete in a grueling 24 hour race in the Rockies. Founded in 1998, the stage was created to give the best mountain bike endurance athletes in the world a venue and atmosphere fitting a world championships. We were proud to have hosted the first ever World 24 Hour Mountain Bike Championships for solo riders up at the Canmore Nordic Centre. Come to compete or just plan to attend to watch and cheer all those gnarly, mud-stained super fit competitors on. *24hoursofadrenalin.com*

Canmore Folk Festival - August Canadian Long Weekend

Folk musicians from around the world land in Canmore in early August (usually the first weekend of August) for a 3-day weekend of awesome entertainment. Pull out your old tie-dye, peace signs, bell-bottoms and funky hats and channel your inner karma. Oh, and if you can, please humanely capture and adopt a Canmore bunny while you're at the festival to help us reduce the population. *canmorefolkfestival.com*

Banff National Park Dragon Boat Festival

Myth meets present-day human strength and stamina at the Banff National Park Dragon Boat Festival. Every August a multitude of colourfully decorated boats take to the waters in Banff in an epic paddle race to the finish line. Come join the pageantry....Prince William and Princess Kate did, so you should too!

Canmore Highland Games Labour Day Weekend

Celebrate everything Scottish while you immerse yourself in the Canmore Highland Games. Highland dancers, pipers, drummers, ethnic foods, a sampling of fine Scottish spirits, a Scottish open-air market and of course, the excitement and pageantry of the highland games competitions themselves will keep everyone happy. They will even have you love'n the Haggis! This wonderful, tasty dish which uses sheep's offal (the bits often discarded like the lungs, heart & liver), are cooked with suet, oatmeal,

The Scott Tartan

Arrrgh laddie!

seasoning and encased in the sheep stomach. Once stitched up, the stuffed stomach is boiled for up to three hours. Yummy!

For more information see *canmorehighlandgames.ca*

Banff Film Festival

Every Oct/Nov Banff hosts the world renown Banff Mountain Film and Book Festival. The world's best mountain films, books, and speakers take the spotlight for nine days so if you're here, don't miss this! Experience the adventure of climbing, mountain expeditions, remote cultures, and the world's last great wild places – all brought to you up close and personal at The Banff Centre. Who knows, my book might even make the competition this year!

Check out banffcentre.ca for all the great events, shows and international cultural activities that happen all year'round.

48 SCENIC DRIVES
Grab the convertible and go

Scenery, possible wildlife sightings, adventure...all from the comfort of your car. What's there not to like?

Hwy 1A East from Canmore to Exshaw

Big horn mountain sheep heaven almost all year 'round. (especially in spring) From Canmore drive east on Hwy 1A out to Exshaw. We've also seen bears, wolves, coyotes, osprey, bald eagles and of course, fabulous scenery!

Lake Minnewanka Loop Just Outside Banff

Mountain sheep, cute smaller critters, elk and a couple of pristine lakes to stop at for a picnic. Two Jacks Lake also is worth a visit en route.

Hwy 1A North from Banff to Lake Louise

Also known as the Bow Valley Parkway, keep a lookout for moose, deer, elk and Castle Mountain views. Visiting Lake Louise once you get there is always worth a stop to take some more scenic photos and check out the historic hotel.

Columbia Ice Fields Parkway

Known as one of the "Top Ten Scenic Drives in the World"! Families of mountain goat families and bears are often seen along this stretch up to the Columbia Ice Fields. Please drive slowly! If you go, you should also take in the Columbia Ice Fields information centre and guided or self-guided tour to see how much the glaciers have receded over time. Don't forget to have a drink of ice cold glacier water just to say that you did.

Please Note: When pulling over to look at and/or photograph wildlife make sure you pull right over to the side shoulder and don't stop too close to the animals. NEVER get out of your vehicle to snap photos and of course, feeding them is totally out of the question. Slow Down! Always observe speed limits to avoid hitting and killing wildlife on our roads – an all too common occurrence here I'm afraid.

49 I'M *HUNGRY!*
No vacation is complete unless you dine out

Impossible to highlight all our great restaurants, the author has eaten at the following establishments in the past year and *"it's all good!"*

Patios for "Alfresco" Dining

Waldhaus at the Banff Springs, 405 Spray Avenue, Banff $$ We often stop and activity to enjoy the views and ambiance on the Walhaus patio. It's a lovely refueling pit stop if you've ridden the Goat Creek Trail from Canmore to Banff and are in need of a pint and some nachos.

The Juniper Hotel, Mount Norquay Road, Banff $$ The Juniper has one of the best views of the valley and Mount Rundle range in Banff.

Canmore Golf & Curling Club 2008 - 8th Avenue $$ Consistently good food combined with fabulous flower garden, water fountain and Mt. views.

Stoney's Grill patio at Silvertip Golf Resort, 2000 Silvertip Trail, Canmore $$ Worth a visit for the great food, stunning golf course setting and to watch golfers try to chip 'n sink their putts on the 18th hole.

Rose & Crown Restaurant & Pub, 749 Railway Avenue, Canmore $$ Quiet and pretty, their shaded patio deck overlooks the wetlands of Policeman's Creek. Also have a kiddie play set out on the deck to keep the little one's happy while you relax and enjoy your meal.

The Iron Goat, 703 Benchlands Trail, Canmore $$ The Iron Goats huge patio overlooks the best Three Sisters Mountain view in town. Heat lamps keep you toasty warm in the evenings.

Best All-Day Breakfast & Family Diners

Craig's Way Station, 1727 Mountain Avenue, Canmore, just off the Trans-Canada Hwy. $$ Family run and operating in the valley for over 25 years, Craig's has become a Canmore icon and is very popular with locals. They can get quite busy on weekends so arrive early to avoid line ups.

Melissa's Missteak, 218 Lynx Street, Banff $$ A Banff icon for 30 years, legendary breakfasts and HUGE pancakes to get you off to a fine start on your vacation.

Pizza Places

Rocky Mountain Flatbread Co., 838 - 10th Street, Canmore $$ Wood oven-fired, custom and unique pizza's – yummy!

Patrinos Steak House and Pub, 1602 Bow Valley Trail, Canmore $$ Family owned and operating in Canmore for more than 20 years, we love their unique and super cheesy square style pizza's. This is the old-timer Canmore hockey teams favourite place too.

The Bear Street Tavern, 211 Bear Street, Banff $$ You'll rave about their delicious and creative pizzas. Take them up on the chili oil or honey as a condiment for your pizza. Atmosphere is comfortable with good tunes that make you want to stay after your meal for another drink.

Ethnic Restaurants

O Bistro, 626 Main Street, Canmore $$ Savoury foods that highlight European, Asian and of course, Canadian accents. Wonderful homemade soups.

The Railway Deli, corner of Benchlands and Bow Valley Trail with parking at the back. $$ Swiss, German, French and European delicacies, fondue, raclette, amazing take out lunch or dinner fare, wonderful marinated meats, cold cuts, breads, cheeses...all so good!

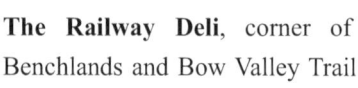

Thai Pagoda, 1306 Bow Valley Trail, Canmore $$ Highly recommended for the attentive service, freshly prepared authentic Thai food and fabulous wine and extensive international beer selections. A favourite – the green curry, their wonderful spring rolls, and the coconut ice cream for dessert.

Elita $$ is located on Railway Ave across from Canmore's new multiplex building (under construction) and off-street parking is available at the left side of the building. Try their red chicken curry, made fresh to order. Elita also boasts a number of vegetarian/vegan and gluten free items on their menu, all with a choice of Mediterranean/Pacific Rim or North American flare.

French Quarter Café, 1005 Cougar Creek Drive, Canmore $$ If you're hankering from some authentic "big easy" New Orleans Cajun and Creole style food, this is it. Seafood gumbo that would make Jimmy Buffett proud.

Balkan Greek Restaurant, 120 Banff Avenue, Banff $$ The Balkan restaurant first fired up its grill on Banff Avenue in1982 by Greek families who still run a festive and fun, authentically delicious Greek establishment today. Greek nights Tues/Thurs are a blast. Smash some dishes and try a belly dance. *Opa!*

Fine Dining for Those Special Occasions (reservations recommended)

Rimrock Resort, 300 Mountain Avenue, Banff $$$$ Winner of the Opentable.com Diner's Choice 2012 award, AAA and Five Diamond awards, the Rimrock is an amazing dining experience. Offering French cuisine with regional accents and combined with Eden's Wine Spectator Best of Award of Excellence and exceptional service, this restaurant really made our evening memorable.

The Trough Dining Co. $$$$, 729B 9th Street (in behind the Canmore Civic Centre) An inspiring and eclectic menu will be sure to reward your taste buds. Delicious desserts.

Rustica Steakhouse at Silvertip $$$$, 2000 Silvertip Trail, Canmore Over the years this has by far been our favourite because of constantly amazing food, succulent AAA Alberta beef, wild game and other innovative creations from a Chef who's truly inspiring. Treat yourself for that special occasion.

Free range elk

Dinner Theatre Fun!

The Cornerstone Dinner Theatre, 125 Kananaskis Way $$$ Don't miss Canmore's only dinner theatre. Enjoy a variety of "Broadway Show" quality entertainment, comedy nights, concerts and their signature Oh Canada Eh! musical that pokes fun at Canadian culture and all us crazy Canucks. Combined with tasty homegrown Canadian comfort food, a night at The Corner is a definite treat for the whole family. We have enjoyed many a performance there. Call for tickets & reservations 403-609-0004 or just book online at their website – atthecorner.ca. The Cornerstone also host weddings, corporate events, Christmas parties etc.

Hello Kitty hams it up

Caffeine Fix Anyone?

Canmore and Banff are home to a great variety of exceptional coffee and tea establishments when you're in need of that caffeine jolt and perhaps some homemade baked goods, soups 'n sandwiches.

The Rocky Mountain Bagel Co., 1306 Bow Valley Trail or at 830 8th (Main) Street, Canmore

Beamers Coffee Bar, 1702 Bow Valley Trail and at 737-7th Avenue in downtown Canmore

Communitea Café, 1001-6th Avenue, Canmore

The Summit, 1001 Cougar Creek Drive, Canmore

Banff, also boasts the roasts. When I'm in Banff I go to **The Banff Tea Company** at 208 Caribou Street for their huge variety of international and local blends. They've also starting importing tempting Olive oils and flavoured vinegars. A portion of all their profits go to worthy charities too.

My Favourite Watering Holes

For those of you 18 and older visitors, you just might hanker for some thirst quenching Canadian brew (which is *wayyy* better than American beer – ha ha). After enjoying a great outdoors day, shoot a game of pool, play darts or just sit'n chill to some live music at the following establishments...

Grizzly Paw Brewing Company, 622 - 8th Street (Main Street) Canmore Experience our town's only microbrew pub that opened back in 1996. The Paw's cleverly named seasonal microbrew's such as "Powder Hound Pilsner" or "Rutting Elk Red" are delicious to sample along with some hearty pub grub. Kids will enjoy their locally made sodas, especially the Root Beer floats. Cozy fireplace patio too.

Canmore Hotel (est. 1888), 738 - 8th Street (Main Street), Canmore The Hotel is a lively part of Canmore's history, and is a local favourite. Pool tables, darts, live entertainment along with great daily lunch specials.

Canmore Legion, Corner of 8th Avenue and Veteran's Way Canmore Support our troops and enjoy some of the cheapest pints of beer in town. They also have pool tables, darts, bingo nights & Canmore Idol events.

Rose & Crown Restaurant & Pub, 749 Railway Avenue Canmore Boasting a large patio that borders the green, serene Policeman's Creek, the R&C has great food, plus occasional live bands on weekends.

The Drake Pub & Inn, 909 Railway Avenue Canmore The Drake deserves a patio honorable mention. Their elevated patio offers a great view of our fabulous July 1st Canada Day parade but arrive early to score a table. They frequently offer good ole rock'n roll live band entertainment most weekends as well.

The Georgetown Inn Miner's Lamp Pub, 1101 Bow Valley Trail Canmore
The cozy fireplace pub boasts the best battered Halibut fish and chips in town and I have to agree. In fine British tradition, many local and European lagers and ales are available to go with your tasty pub grub.

The

Banff Brewing Company, 2nd Floor, 110 Banff Avenue, Banff   The BBC is Banff's only microbrewing company. They have an impressive variety of innovative beer selections and a tempting food menu as well. Enjoy a funky and hip atmosphere as you watch the brewmasters at work while you dine.

50 OFF THE BEATEN PATH
Check out local places that aren't on main street

Get outta town! No really, hop in your car and check out some of our amazing local artists, artisans, chocolatiers, bakeries and eateries

Of Cabbages and Kings Pottery, 129 Bow Meadows Crescent, Canmore If you love pottery, you should visit these folks. Really innovative and functional pottery designs, innovative glaze firing techniques and very reasonable prices.

Hot Glass Studios, Unit #8, 111 Bow Meadows Crescent, Canmore Totally unique and beautiful works of glass art. Call ahead to book a really cool, or should I say "hot", glass blowing demonstration and confirm their hours of operation as they do vary. (403) 609-9333.

Ammonite Gem Co. Ltd., 106 Bow Meadows Crescent, Canmore A "made in Alberta gemstone" Ammonite is made out of ancient fossilized Ammonite sea critters! This is amazing stuff that is only found in Alberta. The beautiful jewelry has all the colours the rainbow in every stone, so Ammonite goes with almost anything. Trust me.

Bernhard's Creative Woodwork Inc. , 4-104 Boulder Crescent, Canmore Beautifully crafted wooden bowls, and *objets d'art* out of unique and fine varieties of hardwood. Great prices here too.

Le Chocolatier, 121, 701 Benchlands Trail, Canmore   John and Belinda outdo themselves with the most amazing and delicious truffles and clever seasonal chocolate creations. Indulge your chocolate cravings whilst enjoying all the health benefits. You know, all of chocolate's antioxidants and flavonoids! They also offer group lessons on how to make your own chocolate creations. Fun!

La Belle Patate, Bay #4, 104 Boulder Crescent, Canmore This little French-Canadian gem is worth a stop to enjoy their amazing "Poutine". A Quebec food staple, Poutine consists of a melange of fresh cut French fries topped with cheese curds, gravy and an assortment of other scrumptious toppings. *C'est bon!*

Fergie's Bakery and Organic Food Convenience Market, 1001 Cougar Creek Drive   Just walking into Fergie's makes you salivate. The smell of fabulous homemade breads, rolls, cinnamon buns, Tourtiere meat and fruit pies will put all thoughts of dieting aside. They also have organic fresh produce plus traditional convenience store items all rolled into one.

A Final Note from the Author

I hope you've enjoyed your experiences with *Out'n About*. So, now that you've had a chance to use this guide, I'd really appreciate hearing from you. How were the directions and time guess estimates? Did you come across any wild life or trail hazards while on your ventures? Were some hikes or suggested activities duds or some that really stood out in your mind as "must-do" fantastic? Is there stuff you think we should include in the next edition? More things in Banff? Farther afield excursions? All comments positive or negative are welcome. (but don't hurt my feelings)

Email me at donnacanmore@gmail.com and tell me your thoughts.

Thanks again for buying my second edition *Out'n About* book! I hope you come back soon to visit and explore more of our wonderful area any time of year. Tell your friends and relatives to visit us too, *eh*!

TTFN,

>D